Travel phrasebooks collection
«Everything Will Be Okay!»

G000070520

PHRASEBOOK

- UKRAINIAN -

THE MOST IMPORTANT PHRASES

This phrasebook contains
the most important
phrases and questions
for basic communication
Everything you need
to survive overseas

By Andrey Taranov

T&P BOOKS

Phrasebook + 1500-word dictionary

English-Ukrainian phrasebook & concise dictionary

By Andrey Taranov

The collection of "Everything Will Be Okay" travel phrasebooks published by T&P Books is designed for people traveling abroad for tourism and business. The phrasebooks contain what matters most - the essentials for basic communication. This is an indispensable set of phrases to "survive" while abroad.

Another section of the book also provides a small dictionary with more than 1,500 useful words arranged alphabetically. The dictionary includes a lot of gastronomic terms and will be helpful when ordering food at a restaurant or buying groceries at the store.

T&P Books Publishing
www.tpbooks.com

ISBN: 978-1-78616-754-5

This book is also available in E-book formats.
Please visit www.tpbooks.com or the major online bookstores.

FOREWORD

The collection of "Everything Will Be Okay" travel phrasebooks published by T&P Books is designed for people traveling abroad for tourism and business. The phrasebooks contain what matters most - the essentials for basic communication. This is an indispensable set of phrases to "survive" while abroad.

This phrasebook will help you in most cases where you need to ask something, get directions, find out how much something costs, etc. It can also resolve difficult communication situations where gestures just won't help.

This book contains a lot of phrases that have been grouped according to the most relevant topics. A separate section of the book also provides a small dictionary with more than 1,500 important and useful words.

Take "Everything Will Be Okay" phrasebook with you on the road and you'll have an irreplaceable traveling companion who will help you find your way out of any situation and teach you to not fear speaking with foreigners.

TABLE OF CONTENTS

T&P Books Publishing

PRONUNCIATION

Letter	Ukrainian example	T&P phonetic alphabet	English example

Vowels

Letter	Ukrainian example	T&P phonetic alphabet	English example
А а	акт	[a]	shorter than in ask
Е е	берет	[e], [ɛ]	absent, pet
Є є	модельєр	[ɛ]	man, bad
И и	ритм	[k]	clock, kiss
І і	компанія	[i]	shorter than in feet
Ї ї	поїзд	[ji]	playing, spying
О о	око	[ɔ]	bottle, doctor
У у	буря	[u]	book
Ю ю	костюм	[ʲu]	cued, cute
Я я	маяк	[ja], [ʲa]	royal

Consonants

Letter	Ukrainian example	T&P phonetic alphabet	English example
Б б	бездна	[b]	baby, book
В в	вікно	[w]	vase, winter
Г г	готель	[h]	between [g] and [h]
Ґ ґ	ґудзик	[g]	game, gold
Д д	дефіс	[d]	day, doctor
Ж ж	жанр	[ʒ]	forge, pleasure
З з	зброя	[z]	zebra, please
Й й	йти	[j]	yes, New York
К к	крок	[k]	clock, kiss
Л л	лев	[l]	lace, people
М м	мати	[m]	magic, milk
Н н	назва	[n]	name, normal
П п	приз	[p]	pencil, private
Р р	радість	[r]	rice, radio
С с	сон	[s]	city, boss
Т т	тир	[t]	tourist, trip
Ф ф	фарба	[f]	face, food
Х х	холод	[h]	home, have
Ц ц	церква	[ts]	cats, tsetse fly
Ч ч	час	[tʃ]	church, French

Letter	Ukrainian example	T&P phonetic alphabet	English example
Ш ш	шуба	[ʃ]	machine, shark
Щ щ	щука	[ɕ]	sheep, shop
ь	камінь	[ʲ]	soft sign - no sound
ъ	ім'я	[ʼ]	hard sign, no sound

LIST OF ABBREVIATIONS

English abbreviations

ab.	-	about
adj	-	adjective
adv	-	adverb
anim.	-	animate
as adj	-	attributive noun used as adjective
e.g.	-	for example
etc.	-	et cetera
fam.	-	familiar
fem.	-	feminine
form.	-	formal
inanim.	-	inanimate
masc.	-	masculine
math	-	mathematics
mil.	-	military
n	-	noun
pl	-	plural
pron.	-	pronoun
sb	-	somebody
sing.	-	singular
sth	-	something
v aux	-	auxiliary verb
vi	-	intransitive verb
vi, vt	-	intransitive, transitive verb
vt	-	transitive verb

Ukrainian abbreviations

ж	-	feminine noun
мн	-	plural
с	-	neuter
ч	-	masculine noun

UKRAINIAN
PHRASEBOOK

This section contains
important phrases that may
come in handy in various
real-life situations.
The phrasebook will help
you ask for directions, clarify
a price, buy tickets, and
order food at a restaurant

T&P Books Publishing

PHRASEBOOK
CONTENTS

T&P Books Publishing

Excuse me, ...

Вибачте, ...
['wibatʃtɛ, ...]

Hello.

Добрий день.
['dɔbrij dɛnʲ.]

Thank you.

Дякую.
['dʲakuʲu.]

Good bye.

До побачення.
[do poˈbatʃɛnʲa.]

Yes.

Так.
[tak.]

No.

Ні.
[ni.]

I don't know.

Я не знаю.
[ja nɛ ˈznaʲu.]

Where? | Where to? | When?

Де? | Куди? | Коли?
[dɛ? | kuˈdɨ? | koˈlɨ?]

I need ...

Мені потрібен ...
[mɛˈni poˈtribɛn ...]

I want ...

Я хочу ...
[ja ˈhɔtʃu ...]

Do you have ...?

У вас є ...?
[u was ˈɛ ...?]

Is there a ... here?

Тут є ...?
[tut ɛ ...?]

May I ...?

Чи можна мені ...?
[tʃi ˈmɔʒna mɛˈni ...?]

..., please (polite request)

Будь ласка
[budʲ ˈlaska]

I'm looking for ...

Я шукаю ...
[ja ʃuˈkaʲu ...]

restroom

туалет
[tuaˈlɛt]

ATM

банкомат
[bankoˈmat]

pharmacy (drugstore)

аптеку
[apˈtɛku]

hospital

лікарню
[liˈkarnʲu]

police station

поліцейську дільницю
[poliˈʦɛjsʲku dilʲˈniʦʲu]

subway

метро
[mɛtˈrɔ]

taxi	**таксі** [tak'si]
train station	**вокзал** [wok'zal]

My name is …	**Мене звуть …** [mɛ'nɛ zwutⁱ …]
What's your name?	**Як вас звуть?** [jak was 'zwutⁱ?]
Could you please help me?	**Допоможіть мені, будь ласка.** [dopomo'ʒitⁱ mɛ'ni, budⁱ 'laska.]
I've got a problem.	**У мене проблема.** [u 'mɛnɛ prob'lɛma.]
I don't feel well.	**Мені погано.** [mɛ'ni po'ɦano.]
Call an ambulance!	**Викличте швидку!** ['wiklitʃtɛ ʃwid'ku!]
May I make a call?	**Чи можна мені зателефонувати?** [tʃi 'mɔʒna mɛ'ni zatɛlɛfonu'wati?]

I'm sorry.	**Прошу вибачення** ['prɔʃu 'wibatʃɛnⁱa]
You're welcome.	**Прошу** ['prɔʃu]

I, me	**я** [ja]
you (inform.)	**ти** [ti]
he	**він** [win]
she	**вона** [wo'na]
they (masc.)	**вони** [wo'nɨ]
they (fem.)	**вони** [wo'nɨ]
we	**ми** [mɨ]
you (pl)	**ви** [wɨ]
you (sg, form.)	**Ви** [wɨ]

ENTRANCE	**ВХІД** [whid]
EXIT	**ВИХІД** ['wihid]
OUT OF ORDER	**НЕ ПРАЦЮЄ** [nɛ pra'tsⁱuɛ]
CLOSED	**ЗАКРИТО** [za'krito]

OPEN

ВІДКРИТО
[wid'krito]

FOR WOMEN

ДЛЯ ЖІНОК
[dlʲa ʒi'nɔk]

FOR MEN

ДЛЯ ЧОЛОВІКІВ
[dlʲa tʃolowi'kiw]

Questions

Where?	**Де?** [dɛ?]
Where to?	**Куди?** [ku'dɨ?]
Where from?	**Звідки?** ['zwidkɨ?]
Why?	**Чому?** [tʃo'mu?]
For what reason?	**Навіщо?** [na'wiɕo?]
When?	**Коли?** [ko'lɨ?]

How long?	**Скільки часу?** ['skilʲkɨ 'tʃasu?]
At what time?	**О котрій?** [o kot'rij?]
How much?	**Скільки коштує?** ['skilʲkɨ 'koʃtuɛ?]
Do you have ...?	**У вас є ...?** [u was 'ɛ ...?]
Where is ...?	**Де знаходиться ...?** [dɛ zna'hodɨtʲsʲa ...?]

What time is it?	**Котра година?** [ko'tra ɦo'dɨna?]
May I make a call?	**Чи можна мені зателефонувати?** [tʃɨ 'moʒna mɛ'ni zatɛlɛfonu'watɨ?]
Who's there?	**Хто там?** [hto tam?]
Can I smoke here?	**Чи можна мені тут палити?** [tʃɨ 'moʒna mɛ'ni tut pa'lɨtɨ?]
May I ...?	**Чи можна мені ...?** [tʃɨ 'moʒna mɛ'ni ...?]

Needs

I'd like ...	**Я б хотів /хотіла/ ...** [ja b ho'tiw /ho'tila/ ...]
I don't want ...	**Я не хочу ...** [ja nɛ 'hotʃu ...]
I'm thirsty.	**Я хочу пити.** [ja 'hotʃu 'piti.]
I want to sleep.	**Я хочу спати.** [ja 'hotʃu 'spati.]

I want ...	**Я хочу ...** [ja 'hotʃu ...]
to wash up	**вмитися** ['wmitisʲa]
to brush my teeth	**почистити зуби** [po'tʃistiti 'zubɨ]
to rest a while	**трохи відпочити** ['trohɨ widpo'tʃiti]
to change my clothes	**переодягнутися** [pɛrɛodʲahʲnutisʲa]

to go back to the hotel	**повернутися в готель** [powɛr'nutisʲa w ɦo'tɛlʲ]
to buy ...	**купити ...** [ku'pitɨ ...]
to go to ...	**з'їздити в ...** ['zʲizdɨtɨ w ...]
to visit ...	**відвідати ...** [wid'widatɨ ...]
to meet with ...	**зустрітися з ...** [zust'ritisʲa z ...]
to make a call	**зателефонувати** [zatɛlɛfonu'watɨ]

I'm tired.	**Я втомився /втомилася/.** [ja wto'miwsʲa /wto'milasʲa/.]
We are tired.	**Ми втомилися.** [mɨ wto'milɨsʲa.]
I'm cold.	**Мені холодно.** [mɛ'ni 'hɔlodno.]
I'm hot.	**Мені спекотно.** [mɛ'ni spɛ'kɔtno.]
I'm OK.	**Мені нормально.** [mɛ'ni nor'malʲno.]

I need to make a call.

Мені треба зателефонувати.
[mɛ'ni 'trɛba zatɛlɛfonu'watɨ.]

I need to go to the restroom.

Мені треба в туалет.
[mɛ'ni 'trɛba w tua'lɛt.]

I have to go.

Мені вже час.
[mɛ'ni wʒɛ ʧas.]

I have to go now.

Мушу вже йти.
['muʃu wʒɛ jtɨ.]

Asking for directions

Excuse me, ...

Вибачте, ...
['wɪbatʃtɛ, ...]

Where is ...?

Де знаходиться ...?
[dɛ zna'hɔditʲsʲa ...?]

Which way is ...?

В якому напрямку знаходиться ...?
[w ja'kɔmu 'napriamku zna'hɔditʲsʲa ...?]

Could you help me, please?

Допоможіть мені, будь ласка.
[dopomo'ʒitʲ mɛ'ni, budʲ 'laska.]

I'm looking for ...

Я шукаю ...
[ja ʃu'kaʲu ...]

I'm looking for the exit.

Я шукаю вихід.
[ja ʃu'kaʲu 'wɪhid.]

I'm going to ...

Я їду в ...
[ja 'idu w ...]

Am I going the right way to ...?

Чи правильно я йду ...?
[tʃi 'prawɪlʲno ja jdu ...?]

Is it far?

Це далеко?
[tsɛ da'lɛko?]

Can I get there on foot?

Чи дійду я туди пішки?
[tʃi dij'du ja tu'di 'piʃki?]

Can you show me on the map?

Покажіть мені на карті, будь ласка.
[poka'ʒitʲ mɛ'ni na 'karti, budʲ 'laska.]

Show me where we are right now.

Покажіть, де ми зараз.
[poka'ʒitʲ, dɛ mɪ 'zaraz.]

Here

Тут
[tut]

There

Там
[tam]

This way

Сюди
[sʲu'di]

Turn right.

Поверніть направо.
[powɛr'nitʲ na'prawo.]

Turn left.

Поверніть наліво.
[powɛr'nitʲ na'liwo.]

first (second, third) turn

перший (другий, третій) поворот
['pɛrʃij ('druhij, 'trɛtij) powo'rɔt]

to the right

направо
[na'prawo]

to the left

наліво
[na'liwo]

Go straight ahead.

Ідіть прямо.
[i'ditʲ 'prʲamo.]

Signs

WELCOME!	**ЛАСКАВО ПРОСИМО** [las'kawo 'prɔsimo]
ENTRANCE	**ВХІД** [whid]
EXIT	**ВИХІД** ['wɨhid]

PUSH	**ВІД СЕБЕ** [wid 'sɛbɛ]
PULL	**ДО СЕБЕ** [do 'sɛbɛ]
OPEN	**ВІДКРИТО** [wid'krito]
CLOSED	**ЗАКРИТО** [za'krito]

FOR WOMEN	**ДЛЯ ЖІНОК** [dlʲa ʒi'nɔk]
FOR MEN	**ДЛЯ ЧОЛОВІКІВ** [dlʲa tʃolowi'kiw]
GENTLEMEN, GENTS (m)	**ЧОЛОВІЧИЙ ТУАЛЕТ** [tʃolo'witʃij tua'lɛt]
WOMEN (f)	**ЖІНОЧИЙ ТУАЛЕТ** [ʒi'nɔtʃij tua'lɛt]

DISCOUNTS	**ЗНИЖКИ** ['zniʒki]
SALE	**РОЗПРОДАЖ** [roz'prɔdaʒ]
FREE	**БЕЗКОШТОВНО** [bɛzkoʃ'towno]
NEW!	**НОВИНКА!** [no'winka!]
ATTENTION!	**УВАГА!** [u'waɦa!]

NO VACANCIES	**МІСЦЬ НЕМАЄ** [mists nɛ'maɛ]
RESERVED	**ЗАРЕЗЕРВОВАНО** [zarɛzɛr'wowano]
ADMINISTRATION	**АДМІНІСТРАЦІЯ** [admini'stratsiʲa]
STAFF ONLY	**ТІЛЬКИ ДЛЯ ПЕРСОНАЛУ** ['tilʲki dlʲa pɛrso'nalu]

BEWARE OF THE DOG!	**ЗЛИЙ СОБАКА** [zlij so'baka]
NO SMOKING!	**НЕ ПАЛИТИ!** [nɛ pa'liti!]
DO NOT TOUCH!	**РУКАМИ НЕ ТОРКАТИСЯ!** [ru'kamɨ nɛ tor'katisʲa!]
DANGEROUS	**НЕБЕЗПЕЧНО** [nɛbɛz'pɛtʃno]
DANGER	**НЕБЕЗПЕКА** [nɛbɛz'pɛka]
HIGH VOLTAGE	**ВИСОКА НАПРУГА** [wɨ'sɔka na'pruɦa]
NO SWIMMING!	**КУПАТИСЯ ЗАБОРОНЕНО** [ku'patisʲa zabo'rɔnɛno]
OUT OF ORDER	**НЕ ПРАЦЮЄ** [nɛ pra'tsʲuɛ]
FLAMMABLE	**ВОГНЕНЕБЕЗПЕЧНО** ['woɦnɛ nɛbɛz'pɛtʃno]
FORBIDDEN	**ЗАБОРОНЕНО** [zabo'rɔnɛno]
NO TRESPASSING!	**ПРОХІД ЗАБОРОНЕНИЙ** [pro'hid zabo'rɔnɛnɨj]
WET PAINT	**ПОФАРБОВАНО** [pofar'bowano]
CLOSED FOR RENOVATIONS	**ЗАКРИТО НА РЕМОНТ** [za'krɨto na rɛ'mɔnt]
WORKS AHEAD	**РЕМОНТНІ РОБОТИ** [rɛ'mɔntni ro'bɔtɨ]
DETOUR	**ОБ'ЇЗД** [ob"izd]

Transportation. General phrases

plane	**літак** [li'tak]
train	**поїзд** ['poizd]
bus	**автобус** [aw'tɔbus]
ferry	**пором** [po'rɔm]
taxi	**таксі** [tak'si]
car	**автомобіль** [awtomo'biˡ]
schedule	**розклад** ['rɔzklad]
Where can I see the schedule?	**Де можна подивитися розклад?** [dɛ 'mɔʒna podiˡ'witisˡa 'rɔzklad?]
workdays (weekdays)	**робочі дні** [ro'bɔʧi dni]
weekends	**вихідні дні** [wihid'ni dni]
holidays	**святкові дні** [swˡat'kɔwi dni]
DEPARTURE	**ВІДПРАВЛЕННЯ** [wid'prawlɛnˡa]
ARRIVAL	**ПРИБУТТЯ** [pribut'tˡa]
DELAYED	**ЗАТРИМУЄТЬСЯ** [za'trimuɛtˡsˡa]
CANCELLED	**ВІДМІНЕНИЙ** [wid'minɛnij]
next (train, etc.)	**наступний** [na'stupnij]
first	**перший** ['pɛrʃij]
last	**останній** [os'tanij]
When is the next ...?	**Коли буде наступний ...?** [ko'li 'budɛ na'stupnij ...?]
When is the first ...?	**Коли відправляється перший ...?** [ko'li widpraw'lˡaɛtˡsˡa 'pɛrʃij ...?]

When is the last ...?

Коли відправляється останній ...?
[ko'lɨ widpraw'lʲaɛtʲsʲa os'tanij ...?]

transfer (change of trains, etc.)

пересадка
[pɛrɛ'sadka]

to make a transfer

зробити пересадку
[zro'bɨtɨ pɛrɛ'sadku]

Do I need to make a transfer?

Чи потрібно мені робити пересадку?
[tʃɨ pot'ribno mɛ'ni ro'bɨtɨ pɛrɛ'sadku?]

Buying tickets

Where can I buy tickets?	**Де я можу купити квитки?** [dɛ ja 'mɔʒu ku'pɨtɨ kwɨt'kɨ?]
ticket	**квиток** [kwɨ'tɔk]
to buy a ticket	**купити квиток** [ku'pɨtɨ kwɨ'tɔk]
ticket price	**вартість квитка** ['wartistʲ kwɨt'ka]

Where to?	**Куди?** [ku'dɨ?]
To what station?	**До якої станції?** [do ja'kɔi 'stanʦɨi?]
I need ...	**Мені потрібно ...** [mɛ'ni po'tribno ...]
one ticket	**один квиток** [o'dɨn kwɨ'tɔk]
two tickets	**два квитки** [dwa kwɨt'kɨ]
three tickets	**три квитки** [trɨ kwɨt'kɨ]

one-way	**в один кінець** [w o'dɨn ki'nɛʦ]
round-trip	**туди і назад** [tu'dɨ i na'zad]
first class	**перший клас** ['pɛrʃɨj klas]
second class	**другий клас** ['druɦɨj klas]

today	**сьогодні** [sʲo'ɦɔdni]
tomorrow	**завтра** ['zawtra]
the day after tomorrow	**післязавтра** [pislʲa'zawtra]
in the morning	**вранці** ['wranʦi]
in the afternoon	**вдень** ['wdɛnʲ]
in the evening	**ввечері** ['wvɛʧɛri]

aisle seat	**місце біля проходу** ['mistsɛ 'bilʲa pro'hɔdu]
window seat	**місце біля вікна** ['mistsɛ 'bilʲa wik'na]
How much?	**Скільки?** ['skilʲki?]
Can I pay by credit card?	**Чи можу я заплатити карткою?** [tʃi 'mɔʒu ja zapla'tɨtɨ 'kartkoʲu?]

Bus

bus	**автобус** [aw'tɔbus]
intercity bus	**міжміський автобус** [miʒmis⁣ʲ'kɨj aw'tɔbus]
bus stop	**автобусна зупинка** [aw'tɔbusna zu'pɨnka]
Where's the nearest bus stop?	**Де найближча автобусна зупинка?** [dɛ najb'liʒʧa aw'tɔbusna zu'pɨnka?]
number (bus ~, etc.)	**номер** ['nɔmɛr]
Which bus do I take to get to ...?	**Який автобус їде до ...?** [ja'kɨj aw'tɔbus 'idɛ do ...?]
Does this bus go to ...?	**Цей автобус їде до ...?** [ʦɛj aw'tɔbus 'idɛ do ...?]
How frequent are the buses?	**Як часто ходять автобуси?** [jak 'ʧasto 'hɔdʲatʲ aw'tɔbusɨ?]
every 15 minutes	**кожні 15 хвилин** ['kɔʒni pʲjatʲnadʦʲatʲ hwɨ'lin]
every half hour	**щопівгодини** [ɕopiwho'dɨnɨ]
every hour	**щогодини** [ɕoho'dɨnɨ]
several times a day	**кілька разів на день** ['kilʲka ra'ziw na dɛnʲ]
... times a day	**... разів на день** [... ra'ziw na 'dɛnʲ]
schedule	**розклад** ['rɔzklad]
Where can I see the schedule?	**Де можна подивитися розклад?** [dɛ 'mɔʒna podɨ'wɨtɨsʲa 'rɔzklad?]
When is the next bus?	**Коли буде наступний автобус?** [ko'lɨ 'budɛ na'stupnɨj aw'tɔbus?]
When is the first bus?	**Коли відправляється перший автобус?** [ko'lɨ widpraw'lʲaɛtʲsʲa 'pɛrʃɨj aw'tɔbus?]
When is the last bus?	**Коли їде останній автобус?** [ko'lɨ 'idɛ os'tannij aw'tɔbus?]

stop	**зупинка** [zu'pɨnka]
next stop	**наступна зупинка** [na'stupna zu'pɨnka]
last stop (terminus)	**кінцева зупинка** [kin'ʦɛwa zu'pɨnka]
Stop here, please.	**Зупиніть тут, будь ласка.** [zupɨ'nitʲ tut, budʲ 'laska.]
Excuse me, this is my stop.	**Дозвольте, це моя зупинка.** [doz'wɔlʲtɛ, ʦɛ mo'ʲa zu'pɨnka.]

Train

train	**поїзд** ['pɔizd]
suburban train	**приміський поїзд** [primisʲ"kij 'pɔizd]
long-distance train	**поїзд далекого прямування** ['pɔizd da'lɛkoɦo prʲamu'wanʲa]
train station	**вокзал** [wok'zal]
Excuse me, where is the exit to the platform?	**Вибачте, де вихід до поїздів?** ['wibatʃtɛ, dɛ 'wiɦid do poiz'diw?]

Does this train go to …?	**Цей поїзд їде до …?** [tsɛj 'pɔizd 'idɛ do …?]
next train	**наступний поїзд** [na'stupnij 'pɔizd]
When is the next train?	**Коли буде наступний поїзд?** [ko'li 'budɛ na'stupnij 'pɔizd?]
Where can I see the schedule?	**Де можна подивитися розклад?** [dɛ 'mɔʒna podi'witisʲa 'rɔzklad?]
From which platform?	**З якої платформи?** [z ja'kɔi plat'fɔrmi?]
When does the train arrive in …?	**Коли поїзд прибуває в …?** [ko'li 'pɔizd pribu'waɛ w …?]

Please help me.	**Допоможіть мені, будь ласка.** [dopomo'ʒitʲ mɛ'ni, budʲ 'laska.]
I'm looking for my seat.	**Я шукаю своє місце.** [ja ʃu'kaʲu swo'ɛ 'mistsɛ.]
We're looking for our seats.	**Ми шукаємо наші місця.** [mi ʃu'kaɛmo 'naʃi mis'tsʲa.]
My seat is taken.	**Моє місце зайняте.** [mo'ɛ 'mistsɛ 'zajnʲatɛ.]
Our seats are taken.	**Наші місця зайняті.** ['naʃi mis'tsʲa 'zajnʲati.]

I'm sorry but this is my seat.	**Вибачте, будь ласка, але це** **моє місце.** ['wibatʃtɛ, budʲ 'laska, a'lɛ tsɛ mo'ɛ 'mistsɛ.]
Is this seat taken?	**Це місце вільне?** [tsɛ 'mistsɛ 'wilʲnɛ?]
May I sit here?	**Можна мені тут сісти?** ['mɔʒna mɛ'ni tut 'sisti?]

On the train. Dialogue (No ticket)

Ticket, please.
Ваш квиток, будь ласка.
[waʃ kwɨˈtɔk, budʲ ˈlaska.]

I don't have a ticket.
У мене немає квитка.
[u ˈmɛnɛ nɛˈmaɛ kwɨtˈka.]

I lost my ticket.
Я загубив /загубила/ свій квиток.
[ja zaɦuˈbɨw /zaɦuˈbɨla/ swij kwɨˈtɔk.]

I forgot my ticket at home.
Я забув /забула/ квиток вдома.
[ja zaˈbuw /zaˈbula/ kwɨˈtɔk ˈwdoma.]

You can buy a ticket from me.
Ви можете купити квиток у мене.
[wɨ ˈmɔʒɛtɛ kuˈpɨtɨ kwɨˈtɔk u ˈmɛnɛ.]

You will also have to pay a fine.
Вам ще доведеться заплатити штраф.
[wam ʃɛ dowɛˈdɛtʲsʲa zaplaˈtɨtɨ ʃtraf.]

Okay.
Добре.
[ˈdɔbrɛ.]

Where are you going?
Куди ви їдете?
[kuˈdɨ wɨ ˈidɛtɛ?]

I'm going to ...
Я їду до ...
[ja ˈidu do ...]

How much? I don't understand.
Скільки? Я не розумію.
[ˈskilʲki? ja nɛ rozuˈmiʲu.]

Write it down, please.
Напишіть, будь ласка.
[napɨˈʃitʲ, budʲ ˈlaska.]

Okay. Can I pay with a credit card?
Добре. Чи можу я заплатити карткою?
[ˈdɔbrɛ. ʧɨ ˈmɔʒu ja zaplaˈtɨtɨ ˈkartkoʲu?]

Yes, you can.
Так, можете.
[tak, ˈmɔʒɛtɛ.]

Here's your receipt.
Ось ваша квитанція.
[osʲ ˈwaʃa kwɨˈtantsiʲa.]

Sorry about the fine.
Шкодую про штраф.
[ʃkoˈduʲu pro ˈʃtraf.]

That's okay. It was my fault.
Це нічого. Це моя вина.
[ʦɛ niˈʧoɦo ʦɛ moˈʲa wɨˈna.]

Enjoy your trip.
Приємної вам поїздки.
[prɨˈɛmnoi wam poˈizdkɨ.]

Taxi

taxi	**таксі** [tak'si]
taxi driver	**таксист** [tak'sist]
to catch a taxi	**зловити таксі** [zlo'witi tak'si]
taxi stand	**стоянка таксі** [sto'ianka tak'si]
Where can I get a taxi?	**Де я можу взяти таксі?** [dɛ ja 'mɔʒu 'wzʲati tak'si?]

to call a taxi	**викликати таксі** ['wiklikati tak'si]
I need a taxi.	**Мені потрібно таксі.** [mɛ'ni po'tribno tak'si.]
Right now.	**Просто зараз.** ['prɔsto 'zaraz.]
What is your address (location)?	**Ваша адреса?** ['waʃa ad'rɛsa?]
My address is ...	**Моя адреса ...** [mo'ʲa ad'rɛsa ...]
Your destination?	**Куди ви поїдете?** [ku'di wi po'idɛtɛ?]

Excuse me, ...	**Вибачте, ...** ['wibatʃtɛ, ...]
Are you available?	**Ви вільні?** [wi 'wilʲni?]
How much is it to get to ...?	**Скільки коштує доїхати до ...?** ['skilʲki 'kɔʃtuɛ do'ihati do ...?]
Do you know where it is?	**Ви знаєте, де це?** [wi 'znaɛtɛ, dɛ ʦɛ?]

Airport, please.	**В аеропорт, будь ласка.** [w aɛro'pɔrt, budʲ 'laska.]
Stop here, please.	**Зупиніться тут, будь ласка.** [zupi'nitʲsʲa tut, budʲ 'laska.]
It's not here.	**Це не тут.** [ʦɛ nɛ tut.]
This is the wrong address.	**Це неправильна адреса.** [ʦɛ nɛ'prawilʲna ad'rɛsa.]
Turn left.	**Зараз наліво.** ['zaraz na'liwo.]

Turn right.	**Зараз направо.** ['zaraz naˈprawo.]
How much do I owe you?	**Скільки я вам винен /винна/?** ['skilʲki ja wam ˈwinɛn /ˈwina/?]
I'd like a receipt, please.	**Дайте мені чек, будь ласка.** ['dajtɛ mɛˈni ʧɛk, budʲ ˈlaska.]
Keep the change.	**Здачі не треба.** ['zdaʧi nɛ ˈtrɛba.]

Would you please wait for me?	**Зачекайте мене, будь ласка.** [zaʧɛˈkajtɛ mɛˈnɛ, budʲ ˈlaska.]
five minutes	**5 хвилин** ['pʲatʲ hwiˈlin]
ten minutes	**10 хвилин** ['dɛsʲatʲ hwiˈlin]
fifteen minutes	**15 хвилин** [pʲatˈnadtsʲatʲ hwiˈlin]
twenty minutes	**20 хвилин** ['dwadtsʲatʲ hwiˈlin]
half an hour	**півгодини** [piwɦoˈdini]

Hotel

Hello.
Добрий день.
['dɔbrij dɛnʲ.]

My name is ...
Мене звуть ...
[mɛ'nɛ zwutʲ ...]

I have a reservation.
Я резервував /резервувала/ номер.
[ja rɛzɛrwu'waw /rɛzɛrwu'wala/ 'nɔmɛr.]

I need ...
Мені потрібен ...
[mɛ'ni po'tribɛn ...]

a single room
одномісний номер
[odno'misnɨj 'nɔmɛr]

a double room
двомісний номер
[dwo'misnɨj 'nɔmɛr]

How much is that?
Скільки він коштує?
['skilʲkɨ win 'kɔʃtuɛ?]

That's a bit expensive.
Це трохи дорого.
[ʦɛ 'trɔhɨ 'dɔroɦo.]

Do you have anything else?
У вас є ще що-небудь?
[u was 'ɛ ɕɛ ɕo-'nɛbudʲ?]

I'll take it.
Я візьму його.
[ja wizʲ'mu ʲo'ɦɔ.]

I'll pay in cash.
Я заплачу готівкою.
[ja zapla'ʧu ɦo'tiwkoʲu.]

I've got a problem.
У мене є проблема.
[u 'mɛnɛ ɛ prob'lɛma.]

My ... is out of order.
У мене не працює ...
[u 'mɛnɛ nɛ pra'ʦʲuɛ ...]

TV
телевізор
[tɛlɛ'wizor]

air conditioner
кондиціонер
[kondɨʦio'nɛr]

tap
кран
[kran]

shower
душ
[duʃ]

sink
раковина
['rakowɨna]

safe
сейф
[sɛjf]

door lock
замок
[za'mɔk]

electrical outlet	**розетка** [ro'zɛtka]
hairdryer	**фен** [fɛn]

I don't have …	**У мене немає …** [u 'mɛnɛ nɛ'maɛ …]
water	**води** [wo'dɨ]
light	**світла** ['switla]
electricity	**електрики** [ɛ'lɛktrɨkɨ]

Can you give me …?	**Чи не можете мені дати …?** [tʃɨ nɛ 'mɔʒɛtɛ mɛ'ni 'datɨ …?]
a towel	**рушник** [ruʃ'nɨk]
a blanket	**ковдру** ['kɔwdru]
slippers	**тапочки** ['tapotʃkɨ]
a robe	**халат** [ha'lat]
shampoo	**шампунь** [ʃam'punʲ]
soap	**мило** ['mɨlo]

I'd like to change rooms.	**Я б хотів /хотіла/ поміняти номер.** [ja b ho'tiw /ho'tila/ pomi'nʲatɨ 'nɔmɛr.]
I can't find my key.	**Я не можу знайти свій ключ.** [ja nɛ 'mɔʒu znaj'tɨ swij 'klʲutʃ.]
Could you open my room, please?	**Відкрийте мій номер, будь ласка.** [wid'krɨjtɛ mij 'nɔmɛr, budʲ 'laska.]
Who's there?	**Хто там?** [hto tam?]
Come in!	**Заходьте!** [za'hɔdʲtɛ!]
Just a minute!	**Одну хвилину!** [od'nu hwɨ'lɨnu!]
Not right now, please.	**Будь ласка, не зараз.** [budʲ 'laska, nɛ 'zaraz.]

Come to my room, please.	**Зайдіть до мене, будь ласка.** [zaj'ditʲ do 'mɛnɛ, budʲ 'laska.]
I'd like to order food service.	**Я хочу зробити замовлення їжі в номер.** [ja 'hɔtʃu zro'bɨtɨ za'mɔwlɛnja 'iʒi w 'nɔmɛr.]
My room number is …	**Мій номер кімнати …** [mij 'nɔmɛr kim'natɨ …]

I'm leaving …

Я їду …
[ja 'idu …]

We're leaving …

Ми їдемо …
[mɨ 'idɛmo …]

right now

зараз
['zaraz]

this afternoon

сьогодні після обіду
[sʲo'ɦɔdni 'pislʲa o'bidu]

tonight

сьогодні ввечері
[sʲo'ɦɔdni 'wvɛtʃɛri]

tomorrow

завтра
['zawtra]

tomorrow morning

завтра вранці
['zawtra 'wrantsi]

tomorrow evening

завтра ввечері
['zawtra 'wvɛtʃɛri]

the day after tomorrow

післязавтра
[pislʲa'zawtra]

I'd like to pay.

Я б хотів /хотіла/ розрахуватися.
[ja b ho'tiw /ho'tila/ rozrahu'watisʲa.]

Everything was wonderful.

Все було чудово.
[wsɛ bu'lo tʃu'dowo.]

Where can I get a taxi?

Де я можу взяти таксі?
[dɛ ja 'mɔʒu 'wzʲatɨ tak'si?]

Would you call a taxi for me, please?

Викличте мені таксі, будь ласка.
['wɨklɨtʃtɛ mɛ'ni tak'si, budʲ 'laska.]

Restaurant

Can I look at the menu, please?
Чи можу я подивитися ваше меню?
[tʃi ˈmɔʒu ja podiˈwitisʲa ˈwaʃɛ mɛˈnʲu?]

Table for one.
Столик для одного.
[ˈstɔlik dlʲa odˈnɔɦo.]

There are two (three, four) of us.
Нас двоє (троє, четверо).
[nas ˈdwɔɛ (ˈtrɔɛ, ˈtʃɛtwɛro).]

Smoking
Для курців
[dlʲa kurˈtsiw]

No smoking
Для некурців
[dlʲa nɛkurˈtsiw]

Excuse me! (addressing a waiter)
Будьте ласкаві!
[ˈbudʲtɛ lasˈkawi!]

menu
меню
[mɛˈnʲu]

wine list
карта вин
[ˈkarta win]

The menu, please.
Меню, будь ласка.
[mɛˈnʲu, budʲ ˈlaska.]

Are you ready to order?
Ви готові зробити замовлення?
[wi ɦoˈtɔwi zroˈbiti zaˈmɔwlɛnʲa?]

What will you have?
Що ви будете замовляти?
[ɕo wi ˈbudɛtɛ zamowˈlʲati?]

I'll have …
Я буду …
[ja ˈbudu …]

I'm a vegetarian.
Я вегетаріанець /вегетаріанка/.
[ja wɛɦɛtariˈanɛts /wɛɦɛtariˈanka/.]

meat
м'ясо
[ˈmʲaso]

fish
риба
[ˈriba]

vegetables
овочі
[ˈɔwotʃi]

Do you have vegetarian dishes?
У вас є вегетаріанські страви?
[u was ˈɛ wɛɦɛtariˈansʲki ˈstrawi?]

I don't eat pork.
Я не їм свинину.
[ja nɛ im swiˈninu.]

He /she/ doesn't eat meat.
Він /вона/ не їсть м'ясо.
[win /woˈna/ nɛ istʲ ˈmʲaso.]

I am allergic to …
У мене алергія на …
[u ˈmɛnɛ alɛrˈɦiʲa na …]

Would you please bring me …

Принесіть мені, будь ласка …
[prinɛ'sitʲ mɛ'ni, budʲ 'laska …]

salt | pepper | sugar

сіль | перець | цукор
[silʲ | 'pɛrɛts | 'tsukor]

coffee | tea | dessert

каву | чай | десерт
['kawu | tʃaj | dɛ'sɛrt]

water | sparkling | plain

воду | з газом | без газу
['wɔdu | z 'ɦazom | bɛz 'ɦazu]

a spoon | fork | knife

ложку | виделку | ніж
['lɔʒku | 'wilku | niʒ]

a plate | napkin

тарілку | серветку
[ta'rilku | sɛr'wɛtku]

Enjoy your meal!

Смачного!
[smatʃ'nɔɦo!]

One more, please.

Принесіть ще, будь ласка.
[prinɛ'sitʲ ɕɛ, budʲ 'laska.]

It was very delicious.

Було дуже смачно.
[bu'lɔ 'duʒɛ 'smatʃno.]

---

check | change | tip

рахунок | здача | чайові
[ra'ɦunok | 'zdatʃa | tʃaʲo'wi]

Check, please.
(Could I have the check, please?)

Рахунок, будь ласка.
[ra'ɦunok, budʲ 'laska.]

Can I pay by credit card?

Чи можу я заплатити карткою?
[tʃi 'mɔʒu ja zapla'titi 'kartkoʲu?]

I'm sorry, there's a mistake here.

Вибачте, тут помилка.
['wibatʃtɛ, tut po'milka.]

Shopping

Can I help you?	Чи можу я вам допомогти? [tʃɨ 'mɔʒu ja wam dopomoɦ'tɨ?]
Do you have ...?	У вас є ...? [u was 'ɛ ...?]
I'm looking for ...	Я шукаю ... [ja ʃu'kaʲu ...]
I need ...	Мені потрібен ... [mɛ'ni po'tribɛn ...]

I'm just looking.	Я просто дивлюся. [ja 'prɔsto 'dɨwlʲusʲa.]
We're just looking.	Ми просто дивимося. [mɨ 'prɔsto 'dɨwɨmosʲa.]
I'll come back later.	Я зайду пізніше. [ja zaj'du piz'niʃɛ.]
We'll come back later.	Ми зайдемо пізніше. [mɨ 'zajdɛmo piz'niʃɛ.]
discounts | sale	знижки | розпродаж ['znɨʒkɨ | roz'prɔdaʒ]

Would you please show me ...	Покажіть мені, будь ласка ... [poka'ʒitʲ mɛ'ni, budʲ 'laska ...]
Would you please give me ...	Дайте мені, будь ласка ... ['dajtɛ mɛ'ni, budʲ 'laska ...]
Can I try it on?	Чи можна мені це приміряти? [tʃɨ 'mɔʒna mɛ'ni tsɛ prɨ'mirʲatɨ?]
Excuse me, where's the fitting room?	Вибачте, де примірювальна? ['wɨbatʃtɛ, dɛ prɨ'mirʲuwalʲna?]
Which color would you like?	Який колір ви хочете? [ja'kij 'kolir wɨ 'hotʃɛtɛ?]
size | length	розмір | зріст ['rɔzmir | zrist]
How does it fit?	Підійшло? [pidij'ʃlo?]

How much is it?	Скільки це коштує? ['skilʲkɨ tsɛ 'koʃtuɛ?]
That's too expensive.	Це занадто дорого. [tsɛ za'nadto 'dɔroɦo.]
I'll take it.	Я візьму це. [ja wizʲ'mu tsɛ.]
Excuse me, where do I pay?	Вибачте, де каса? ['wɨbatʃtɛ, dɛ 'kasa?]

Will you pay in cash or credit card?	**Як ви будете платити? Готівкою чи кредиткою?** [jak wɨ 'budɛtɛ pla'tɨtɨ? ɦo'tiwkoʲu ʧɨ krɛ'dɨtkoʲu?]
In cash | with credit card	**готівкою | карткою** [ɦo'tiwkoʲu | 'kartkoʲu]

Do you want the receipt?	**Вам потрібен чек?** [wam po'tribɛn ʧɛk?]
Yes, please.	**Так, будьте ласкаві.** [tak, 'budʲtɛ las'kawi.]
No, it's OK.	**Ні, не потрібно. Дякую.** [ni, nɛ po'tribno. 'dʲakuʲu.]
Thank you. Have a nice day!	**Дякую. На все добре!** ['dʲakuʲu. na wsɛ 'dɔbrɛ.]

In town

Excuse me, please.	**Вибачте, будь ласка ...** ['wɨbatʃtɛ, budʲ 'laska ...]
I'm looking for ...	**Я шукаю ...** [ja ʃu'kaʲu ...]

the subway	**метро** [mɛt'rɔ]
my hotel	**свій готель** [swij ɦo'tɛlʲ]
the movie theater	**кінотеатр** [kinotɛ'atr]
a taxi stand	**стоянку таксі** [stoʲanku tak'si]

an ATM	**банкомат** [banko'mat]
a foreign exchange office	**обмін валют** ['ɔbmin wa'lʲut]
an internet café	**інтернет-кафе** [intɛr'nɛt-ka'fɛ]
... street	**вулицю ...** ['wulɨtsʲu ...]
this place	**ось це місце** [osʲ tsɛ 'mistsɛ]

Do you know where ... is?	**Чи не знаєте Ви, де знаходиться ...?** [tʃɨ nɛ 'znaɛtɛ wɨ, dɛ zna'ɦodɨtsʲa ...?]
Which street is this?	**Як називається ця вулиця?** [jak nazɨ'waɛtsʲa tsʲa 'wulɨtsʲa?]
Show me where we are right now.	**Покажіть, де ми зараз.** [poka'ʒitʲ, dɛ mɨ 'zaraz.]

Can I get there on foot?	**Я дійду туди пішки?** [ja dij'du tu'dɨ 'piʃkɨ?]
Do you have a map of the city?	**У вас є карта міста?** [u was 'ɛ 'karta 'mista?]

How much is a ticket to get in?	**Скільки коштує вхідний квиток?** ['skilʲkɨ 'koʃtuɛ whid'nɨj kwɨ'tɔk?]
Can I take pictures here?	**Чи можна тут фотографувати?** [tʃɨ 'mɔʒna tut fotoɦrafu'watɨ?]
Are you open?	**Ви відкриті?** [wɨ widk'rɨti?]

When do you open?

О котрій ви відкриваєтесь?
[o kot'rij wɨ widkrɨ'waɛtɛsʲ?]

When do you close?

До котрої години ви працюєте?
[do ko'trɔi ɦo'dɨnɨ wɨ pra'ʦʲuɛtɛ?]

Money

money	гроші
	['ɦrɔʃi]
cash	готівкові гроші
	[ɦotiw'kɔwi 'ɦrɔʃi]
paper money	паперові гроші
	[papɛ'rɔwi 'ɦrɔʃi]
loose change	дрібні гроші
	[drib'ni 'ɦrɔʃi]
check | change | tip	рахунок | здача | чайові
	[ra'ɦunok | 'zdatʃa | tʃaʲo'wi]

credit card	кредитна картка
	[krɛ'ditna 'kartka]
wallet	гаманець
	[ɦama'nɛts]
to buy	купувати
	[kupu'watiʲ]
to pay	платити
	[pla'titiʲ]
fine	штраф
	['ʃtraf]
free	безкоштовно
	[bɛzkoʃ'tɔwno]

Where can I buy ...?	Де я можу купити ...?
	[dɛ ja 'mɔʒu ku'pitiʲ ...?]
Is the bank open now?	Чи відкритий зараз банк?
	[tʃiʲ wid'kritiʲj 'zaraz bank?]
When does it open?	О котрій він відкривається?
	[o kot'rij win widkriʲ'waɛtʲsʲa?]
When does it close?	До котрої години він працює?
	[do ko'trɔi ɦo'diniʲ win pra'tsʲuɛ?]

How much?	Скільки?
	['skilʲki?]
How much is this?	Скільки це коштує?
	['skilʲkiʲ tsɛ 'koʃtuɛ?]
That's too expensive.	Це занадто дорого.
	[tsɛ za'nadto 'dɔroɦo.]

Excuse me, where do I pay?	Вибачте, де каса?
	['wiʲbatʃtɛ, dɛ 'kasa?]
Check, please.	Рахунок, будь ласка.
	[ra'ɦunok, budʲ 'laska.]

Can I pay by credit card?

Чи можу я заплатити карткою?
[tʃɨ 'mɔʒu ja zapla'tɨtɨ 'kartkoʲu?]

Is there an ATM here?

Тут є банкомат?
[tut ɛ banko'mat?]

I'm looking for an ATM.

Мені потрібен банкомат.
[mɛ'ni po'tribɛn banko'mat.]

I'm looking for a foreign exchange office.

Я шукаю обмін валют.
[ja ʃu'kaʲu 'ɔbmin wa'lʲut.]

I'd like to change …

Я б хотів /хотіла/ поміняти …
[ja b ho'tiw /ho'tila/ pomi'nʲatɨ …]

What is the exchange rate?

Який курс обміну?
[ja'kij kurs 'ɔbminu?]

Do you need my passport?

Вам потрібен мій паспорт?
[wam po'tribɛn mij 'pasport?]

Time

What time is it?	**Котра година?** [ko'tra ɦo'dɪna?]
When?	**Коли?** [ko'lɪ?]
At what time?	**О котрій?** [o kot'rij?]
now | later | after ...	**зараз | пізніше | після ...** ['zaraz | piz'niʃɛ | 'pislʲa ...]
one o'clock	**перша година дня** ['pɛrʃa ɦo'dɪna dnʲa]
one fifteen	**п'ятнадцять на другу** [pʲat'nadtsʲatʲ na 'druɦu]
one thirty	**половина другої** [polo'wɪna 'druɦoi]
one forty-five	**за п'ятнадцять друга** [za pʲat'nattsʲatʲ 'druɦa]
one | two | three	**один | два | три** [o'dɪn | dwa | trɪ]
four | five | six	**чотири | п'ять | шість** [tʃo'tɪrɪ | 'pʲatʲ | ʃistʲ]
seven | eight | nine	**сім | вісім | дев'ять** [sim | 'wisim | 'dɛwʲatʲ]
ten | eleven | twelve	**десять | одинадцять | дванадцять** ['dɛsʲatʲ | odɪ'nadtsʲatʲ | dwa'nadtsʲatʲ]
in ...	**через ...** ['tʃɛrɛz ...]
five minutes	**5 хвилин** ['pʲatʲ hwɪ'lɪn]
ten minutes	**10 хвилин** ['dɛsʲatʲ hwɪ'lɪn]
fifteen minutes	**15 хвилин** [pʲat'nadtsʲatʲ hwɪ'lɪn]
twenty minutes	**20 хвилин** ['dwadtsʲatʲ hwɪ'lɪn]
half an hour	**півгодини** [piwɦo'dɪnɪ]
an hour	**одна година** [od'na ɦo'dɪna]
in the morning	**вранці** ['wrantsi]
early in the morning	**рано вранці** ['rano 'wrantsi]

this morning	**сьогодні вранці** [sʲoˈhɔdni ˈwranʦi]
tomorrow morning	**завтра вранці** [ˈzawtra ˈwranʦi]

in the middle of the day	**в обід** [w oˈbid]
in the afternoon	**після обіду** [ˈpislʲa oˈbidu]
in the evening	**ввечері** [ˈwvɛʧɛri]
tonight	**сьогодні ввечері** [sʲoˈhɔdni ˈwvɛʧɛri]

at night	**вночі** [wnoˈʧi]
yesterday	**вчора** [ˈwʧɔra]
today	**сьогодні** [sʲoˈhɔdni]
tomorrow	**завтра** [ˈzawtra]
the day after tomorrow	**післязавтра** [pislʲaˈzawtra]

What day is it today?	**Який сьогодні день?** [jaˈkij sʲoˈhɔdni dɛnʲ?]
It's ...	**Сьогодні ...** [sʲoˈhɔdni ...]
Monday	**понеділок** [ponɛˈdilok]
Tuesday	**вівторок** [wiwˈtɔrok]
Wednesday	**середа** [sɛrɛˈda]

Thursday	**четвер** [ʧɛtˈwɛr]
Friday	**п'ятниця** [ˈpʲatniʦʲa]
Saturday	**субота** [suˈbɔta]
Sunday	**неділя** [nɛˈdilʲa]

Greetings. Introductions

Hello.
Добрий день.
['dɔbrij dɛnʲ.]

Pleased to meet you.
Радий /рада/ з вами познайомитися.
['radij /'rada/ z 'wamɨ pozna'jɔmɨtɨsʲa.]

Me too.
Я теж.
[ja tɛʒ.]

I'd like you to meet ...
Знайомтеся. Це ...
[zna'jɔmtɛsʲa. tsɛ ...]

Nice to meet you.
Дуже приємно.
['duʒɛ prɨ'ɛmno.]

How are you?
Як ви? Як у вас справи?
[jak wɨ? jak u was 'sprawɨ?]

My name is ...
Мене звуть ...
[mɛ'nɛ zwutʲ ...]

His name is ...
Його звуть ...
[ʲo'fʲɔ zwutʲ ...]

Her name is ...
Її звуть ...
[iɨ 'zwutʲ ...]

What's your name?
Як вас звуть?
[jak was 'zwutʲ?]

What's his name?
Як його звуть?
[jak ʲo'fʲɔ zwutʲ?]

What's her name?
Як її звуть?
[jak iɨ 'zwutʲ?]

What's your last name?
Яке ваше прізвище?
[ja'kɛ 'waʃɛ 'prizwɨɕɛ?]

You can call me ...
Називайте мене ...
[nazɨ'wajtɛ mɛ'nɛ ...]

Where are you from?
Звідки ви?
['zwidkɨ wɨ?]

I'm from ...
Я з ...
[ja z ...]

What do you do for a living?
Ким ви працюєте?
[kɨm wɨ pra'tsʲuɛtɛ?]

Who is this?
Хто це?
[hto tsɛ?]

Who is he?
Хто він?
[hto win?]

Who is she?
Хто вона?
[hto wo'na?]

Who are they?	**Хто вони?** [hto wo'nɪ?]
This is ...	**Це ...** [ʦɛ ...]
my friend (masc.)	**мій друг** [mij druɦ]
my friend (fem.)	**моя подруга** [mo'ʲa 'pɔdruɦa]
my husband	**мій чоловік** [mij ʧolo'wik]
my wife	**моя дружина** [mo'ʲa dru'ʒɪna]

my father	**мій батько** [mij 'batʲko]
my mother	**моя мама** [mo'ʲa 'mama]
my brother	**мій брат** [mij brat]
my sister	**моя сестра** [mo'ʲa sɛst'ra]
my son	**мій син** [mij sɪn]
my daughter	**моя дочка** [mo'ʲa doʧ'ka]

This is our son.	**Це наш син.** [ʦɛ naʃ sɪn.]
This is our daughter.	**Це наша дочка.** [ʦɛ 'naʃa doʧ'ka.]
These are my children.	**Це мої діти.** [ʦɛ mo'i 'ditɪ.]
These are our children.	**Це наші діти.** [ʦɛ 'naʃi 'ditɪ.]

Farewells

Good bye!	**До побачення!** [do po'batʃɛnʲa!]
Bye! (inform.)	**Бувай!** [bu'waj!]
See you tomorrow.	**До завтра.** [do 'zawtra.]
See you soon.	**До зустрічі.** [do 'zustritʃi.]
See you at seven.	**Зустрінемось о сьомій.** [zust'rinɛmosʲ o 'sʲɔmij.]
Have fun!	**Розважайтеся!** [rozwa'ʒajtɛsʲa!]
Talk to you later.	**Поговоримо пізніше.** [poɦo'worɨmo piz'niʃɛ.]
Have a nice weekend.	**Вдалих вихідних.** ['wdalɨh wɨhid'nɨh.]
Good night.	**На добраніч.** [na do'branitʃ.]
It's time for me to go.	**Мені вже час.** [mɛ'ni wʒɛ tʃas.]
I have to go.	**Мушу йти.** ['muʃu jtɨ.]
I will be right back.	**Я зараз повернусь.** [ja 'zaraz powɛr'nusʲ.]
It's late.	**Вже пізно.** [wʒɛ 'pizno.]
I have to get up early.	**Мені рано вставати.** [mɛ'ni 'rano wsta'watɨ.]
I'm leaving tomorrow.	**Я завтра від'їжджаю.** [ja 'zawtra widʲiʒ'dʒaʲu.]
We're leaving tomorrow.	**Ми завтра від'їжджаємо.** [mɨ 'zawtra widʲiʒ'dʒaɛmo.]
Have a nice trip!	**Щасливої поїздки!** [ɕas'lɨwoi po'izdkɨ!]
It was nice meeting you.	**Було приємно з вами познайомитися.** [bu'lɔ prɨ'ɛmno z 'wamɨ pozna'jɔmɨtɨsʲa.]

It was nice talking to you.	**Було приємно з вами поспілкуватися.** [bu'lɔ pri'ɛmno z 'wamɨ pospilku'watisʲa.]
Thanks for everything.	**Дякую за все.** ['dʲakuʲu za wsɛ.]

I had a very good time.	**Я чудово провів /провела/ час.** [ja tʃu'dɔwo pro'wiw /prowɛ'la/ tʃas.]
We had a very good time.	**Ми чудово провели час.** [mɨ tʃu'dɔwo prowɛ'lɨ tʃas.]
It was really great.	**Все було чудово.** [wsɛ bu'lɔ tʃu'dɔwo.]
I'm going to miss you.	**Я буду сумувати.** [ja 'budu sumu'watɨ.]
We're going to miss you.	**Ми будемо сумувати.** [mɨ 'budɛmo sumu'watɨ.]

Good luck!	**Успіхів! Щасливо!** ['uspihiw! ɕas'lɨwo!]
Say hi to ...	**Передавайте вітання ...** [pɛrɛda'wajtɛ wi'tanʲa ...]

Foreign language

I don't understand.	**Я не розумію.** [ja nɛ rozu'miʲu.]
Write it down, please.	**Напишіть це, будь ласка.** [napiʲʃitʲ ʦɛ, budʲ 'laska.]
Do you speak …?	**Ви знаєте …?** [wɨ 'znaɛtɛ …?]

I speak a little bit of …	**Я трохи знаю …** [ja 'trɔhɨ znaʲu …]
English	**англійська** [anɦ'lijsʲka]
Turkish	**турецька** [tu'rɛʦka]
Arabic	**арабська** [a'rabsʲka]
French	**французька** [fran'ʦuzʲka]

German	**німецька** [ni'mɛʦka]
Italian	**італійська** [ita'lijsʲka]
Spanish	**іспанська** [is'pansʲka]
Portuguese	**португальська** [portu'ɦalʲsʲka]
Chinese	**китайська** [kɨ'tajsʲka]
Japanese	**японська** [ja'pɔnsʲka]

Can you repeat that, please.	**Повторіть, будь ласка.** [powto'ritʲ, budʲ 'laska.]
I understand.	**Я розумію.** [ja rozu'miʲu.]
I don't understand.	**Я не розумію.** [ja nɛ rozu'miʲu.]
Please speak more slowly.	**Говоріть повільніше, будь ласка.** [ɦowo'ritʲ po'wilʲniʃɛ, 'budʲ 'laska.]

| Is that correct? (Am I saying it right?) | **Це правильно?**
[ʦɛ 'prawɨlʲno?] |
| What is this? (What does this mean?) | **Що це?**
[ɕo 'ʦɛ?] |

Apologies

Excuse me, please.
Вибачте, будь ласка.
['wɨbatʃtɛ, budʲ 'laska.]

I'm sorry.
Мені шкода.
[mɛ'ni 'ʃkɔda.]

I'm really sorry.
Мені дуже шкода.
[mɛ'ni 'duʒɛ 'ʃkɔda.]

Sorry, it's my fault.
Винен /Винна/, це моя вина.
['wɨnɛn /'wɨna/ , ʦɛ mo'ʲa wɨ'na.]

My mistake.
Моя помилка.
[mo'ʲa po'mɨlka.]

May I ...?
Чи можу я ...?
[ʧɨ 'mɔʒu ja ...?]

Do you mind if I ...?
Ви не заперечуватимете, якщо я ...?
[wɨ nɛ zapɛ'rɛʧuwatɨmɛtɛ, jak'ɕɔ ja ...?]

It's OK.
Нічого страшного.
[ni'ʧɔɦo straʃ'nɔɦo.]

It's all right.
Все гаразд.
[wsɛ ɦa'razd.]

Don't worry about it.
Не турбуйтесь.
[nɛ tur'bujtɛsʲ.]

Agreement

Yes.	**Так.** [tak.]
Yes, sure.	**Так, звичайно.** [tak, zwɨ'ʧajno.]
OK (Good!)	**Добре!** ['dɔbrɛ!]
Very well.	**Дуже добре.** ['duʒɛ 'dɔbrɛ.]
Certainly!	**Звичайно!** [zwɨ'ʧajno!]
I agree.	**Я згідний /згідна/.** [ja 'zɦidnɨj /'zɦidna/.]
That's correct.	**Вірно.** ['wirno.]
That's right.	**Правильно.** ['prawɨlʲno.]
You're right.	**Ви праві.** [wɨ pra'wi.]
I don't mind.	**Я не заперечую.** [ja nɛ zapɛ'rɛʧuʲu.]
Absolutely right.	**Абсолютно вірно.** [abso'lʲutno 'wirno.]
It's possible.	**Це можливо.** [ʦɛ moʒ'lɨwo.]
That's a good idea.	**Це гарна думка.** [ʦɛ 'ɦarna 'dumka.]
I can't say no.	**Не можу відмовити.** [nɛ 'mɔʒu wid'mɔwɨtɨ.]
I'd be happy to.	**Буду радий /рада/.** ['budu 'radɨj /'rada/.]
With pleasure.	**Із задоволенням.** [iz zado'wɔlɛnjam.]

Refusal. Expressing doubt

No.
Ні.
[ni.]

Certainly not.
Звичайно, ні.
[zwɨ'ʧajno, ni.]

I don't agree.
Я не згідний /згідна/.
[ja nɛ 'zɦidnɨj /'zɦidna/.]

I don't think so.
Я так не думаю.
[ja tak nɛ 'dumaʲu.]

It's not true.
Це неправда.
[ʦɛ nɛ'prawda.]

You are wrong.
Ви неправі.
[wɨ nɛpra'wi.]

I think you are wrong.
Я думаю, що ви неправі.
[ja 'dumaʲu, ɕo wɨ nɛpra'wi.]

I'm not sure.
Не впевнений /впевнена/.
[nɛ 'wpɛwnɛnɨj /'wpɛwnɛna/.]

It's impossible.
Це неможливо.
[ʦɛ nɛmoʒ'lɨwo.]

Nothing of the kind (sort)!
Нічого подібного!
[ni'ʧoɦo po'dibnoɦo!]

The exact opposite.
Навпаки!
[nawpa'kɨ!]

I'm against it.
Я проти.
[ja 'protɨ.]

I don't care.
Мені все одно.
[mɛ'ni wsɛ od'nɔ.]

I have no idea.
Гадки не маю.
['ɦadkɨ nɛ 'maʲu.]

I doubt it.
Сумніваюся, що це так.
[sumni'waʲusʲa, ɕo ʦɛ tak.]

Sorry, I can't.
Вибачте, я не можу.
['wɨbaʧtɛ, ja nɛ 'mɔʒu.]

Sorry, I don't want to.
Вибачте, я не хочу.
['wɨbaʧtɛ, ja nɛ 'hɔʧu.]

Thank you, but I don't need this.
Дякую, мені це не потрібно.
['dʲakuʲu, mɛ'ni ʦɛ nɛ pot'ribno.]

It's getting late.
Вже пізно.
[wʒɛ 'pizno.]

I have to get up early.

Мені рано вставати.
[mɛˈni ˈrano wstaˈwatɨ.]

I don't feel well.

Я погано себе почуваю.
[ja poˈɦano sɛˈbɛ potʃuˈwaʲu.]

Expressing gratitude

Thank you.	**Дякую.** [ˈdʲakuʲu.]
Thank you very much.	**Дуже дякую.** [ˈduʒɛ ˈdʲakuʲu.]
I really appreciate it.	**Дуже вдячний /вдячна/.** [ˈduʒɛ ˈwdʲatʃnʲij /ˈwdʲatʃna/.]
I'm really grateful to you.	**Я вам вдячний /вдячна/.** [ja wam ˈwdʲatʃnʲij /ˈwdʲatʃna/.]
We are really grateful to you.	**Ми Вам вдячні.** [mɨ wam ˈwdʲatʃni.]

Thank you for your time.	**Дякую, що витратили час.** [ˈdʲakuʲu, ɕo ˈwitratili tʃas.]
Thanks for everything.	**Дякую за все.** [ˈdʲakuʲu za wsɛ.]
Thank you for …	**Дякую за …** [ˈdʲakuʲu za …]
your help	**вашу допомогу** [ˈwaʃu dopoˈmɔɦu]
a nice time	**гарний час** [ˈɦarnʲij tʃas]

a wonderful meal	**чудову їжу** [tʃuˈdɔwu ˈiʒu]
a pleasant evening	**приємний вечір** [priˈɛmnʲij ˈwɛtʃir]
a wonderful day	**чудовий день** [tʃuˈdɔwɨj dɛnʲ]
an amazing journey	**цікаву екскурсію** [tsiˈkawu ɛksˈkursiʲu]

Don't mention it.	**Нема за що.** [nɛˈma za ɕo.]
You are welcome.	**Не варто дякувати.** [nɛ ˈwarto ˈdʲakuwati.]
Any time.	**Завжди будь ласка.** [zaˈwʒdɨ budʲ ˈlaska.]
My pleasure.	**Був радий /Була рада/ допомогти.** [buw ˈradɨj /buˈla ˈrada/ dopoˈmoɦtɨ.]
Forget it.	**Забудьте. Все гаразд.** [zaˈbudʲtɛ wsɛ ɦaˈrazd.]
Don't worry about it.	**Не турбуйтесь.** [nɛ turˈbujtɛsʲ.]

Congratulations. Best wishes

Congratulations!
Вітаю!
[wi'ta^ju!]

Happy birthday!
З Днем народження!
[z dnɛm na'rɔdʒɛnʲa!]

Merry Christmas!
Веселого Різдва!
[wɛ'sɛloɦo rizd'wa!]

Happy New Year!
З Новим роком!
[z no'wɨm 'rɔkom!]

Happy Easter!
Зі Світлим Великоднем!
[zi 'switlɨm wɛ'lɨkodnɛm!]

Happy Hanukkah!
Щасливої Хануки!
[ças'lɨwoi ha'nukɨ!]

I'd like to propose a toast.
У мене є тост.
[u 'mɛnɛ ɛ tost.]

Cheers!
За ваше здоров'я!
[za 'waʃɛ zdo'rɔw^ja]

Let's drink to ...!
Вип'ємо за ...!
['wɨp^jɛmo za ...!]

To our success!
За наш успіх!
[za naʃ 'uspih!]

To your success!
За ваш успіх!
[za waʃ 'uspih!]

Good luck!
Успіхів!
['uspihiw!]

Have a nice day!
Гарного вам дня!
['ɦarnoɦo wam dnʲa!]

Have a good holiday!
Гарного вам відпочинку!
['ɦarnoɦo wam widpo'tʃɨnku!]

Have a safe journey!
Вдалої поїздки!
['wdaloi po'izdkɨ!]

I hope you get better soon!
Бажаю вам швидкого одужання!
[ba'ʒa^ju wam ʃwɨd'kɔɦo o'duʒanʲa!]

Socializing

Why are you sad?

Чому ви засмучені?
[tʃɔ'mu wɨ zas'mutʃɛni?]

Smile! Cheer up!

Посміхніться!
[posmih'nitʲsʲa!]

Are you free tonight?

Ви не зайняті сьогодні ввечері?
[wɨ nɛ 'zajnʲati sʲo'ɦɔdni 'wwɛtʃɛri?]

May I offer you a drink?

Чи можу я запропонувати вам випити?
[tʃɨ 'mɔʒu ja zaproponu'watɨ wam 'wɨpɨti?]

Would you like to dance?

Чи не хочете потанцювати?
[tʃɨ nɛ 'hɔtʃɛtɛ potantsʲu'watɨ?]

Let's go to the movies.

Може сходимо в кіно?
['mɔʒɛ 'shɔdɨmo w ki'nɔ?]

May I invite you to ...?

Чи можна запросити вас в ...?
[tʃɨ 'mɔʒna zapro'sɨti was w ...?]

a restaurant

ресторан
[rɛsto'ran]

the movies

кіно
[ki'nɔ]

the theater

театр
[tɛ'atr]

go for a walk

на прогулянку
[na pro'ɦulʲanku]

At what time?

О котрій?
[o kot'rij?]

tonight

сьогодні ввечері
[sʲo'ɦɔdni 'wwɛtʃɛri]

at six

о 6 годині
[o 'ʃɔstij ɦo'dɨni]

at seven

о 7 годині
[o 'sʲɔmij ɦo'dɨni]

at eight

о 8 годині
[o 'wɔsʲmij ɦo'dɨni]

at nine

о 9 годині
[o dɛ'wʲatij ɦo'dɨni]

Do you like it here?

Вам тут подобається?
[wam tut po'dobaɛtʲsʲa?]

Are you here with someone?

Ви тут з кимось?
[wɨ tut z 'kɨmosʲ?]

I'm with my friend.

Я з другом /подругою/.
[ja z 'druɦom /'pɔdruɦoʲu/.]

I'm with my friends.

Я з друзями.
[ja z 'druzʲamɨ.]

No, I'm alone.

Я один /одна/.
[ja o'dɨn /od'na/.]

Do you have a boyfriend?

У тебе є приятель?
[u 'tɛbɛ ɛ 'prɨjatɛlʲ?]

I have a boyfriend.

У мене є друг.
[u 'mɛnɛ ɛ druɦ.]

Do you have a girlfriend?

У тебе є подружка?
[u 'tɛbɛ ɛ 'pɔdruʒka?]

I have a girlfriend.

У мене є дівчина.
[u 'mɛnɛ ɛ 'diwtʃɨna.]

Can I see you again?

Ми ще зустрінемося?
[mɨ ɕɛ zu'strinɛmosʲa?]

Can I call you?

Чи можна тобі подзвонити?
[tʃɨ 'mɔʒna to'bi zatɛlɛfonu'watɨ?]

Call me. (Give me a call.)

Подзвони мені.
[podzwo'nɨ mɛ'ni.]

What's your number?

Який у тебе номер?
[ja'kɨj u 'tɛbɛ 'nomɛr?]

I miss you.

Я сумую за тобою.
[ja su'muʲu za to'boʲu.]

You have a beautiful name.

У вас дуже гарне ім'я.
[u was 'duʒɛ 'ɦarnɛ i'mʲʲa.]

I love you.

Я тебе кохаю.
[ja tɛbɛ ko'haʲu.]

Will you marry me?

Виходь за мене.
[wɨ'hɔdʲ za 'mɛnɛ.]

You're kidding!

Ви жартуєте!
[wɨ ʒar'tuɛtɛ!]

I'm just kidding.

Я просто жартую.
[ja 'prɔsto ʒar'tuʲu.]

Are you serious?

Ви серйозно?
[wɨ sɛr'jɔzno?]

I'm serious.

Я серйозно.
[ja sɛr'jɔzno.]

Really?!

Справді?!
['sprawdi?!]

It's unbelievable!

Це неймовірно!
[tsɛ nɛjmo'wirno]

I don't believe you.

Я вам не вірю.
[ja wam nɛ 'wirʲu.]

I can't.

Я не можу.
[ja nɛ 'mɔʒu.]

I don't know.

Я не знаю.
[ja nɛ 'znaʲu.]

I don't understand you.	**Я вас не розумію.** [ja was nɛ rozu'mi^ju.]
Please go away.	**Ідіть, будь ласка.** [i'dit^j, bud^j 'laska.]
Leave me alone!	**Залиште мене в спокої!** [za'liʃtɛ mɛ'nɛ w 'spɔkoi!]
I can't stand him.	**Я його терпіти не можу.** [ja ^jo'ɦɔ tɛr'piti nɛ 'mɔʒu.]
You are disgusting!	**Ви огидні!** [wɨ o'ɦɨdni!]
I'll call the police!	**Я викличу поліцію!** [ja 'wɨklɨtʃu po'litsɨ^ju!]

Sharing impressions. Emotions

I like it.	**Мені це подобається.** [mɛ'ni tsɛ po'dɔbaɛtʲsʲa.]
Very nice.	**Дуже мило.** ['duʒɛ 'mіɫo.]
That's great!	**Це чудово!** [tsɛ ʧu'dɔwo!]
It's not bad.	**Це непогано.** [tsɛ nɛpo'ɦano.]

I don't like it.	**Мені це не подобається.** [mɛ'ni tsɛ nɛ po'dɔbaɛtʲsʲa.]
It's not good.	**Це недобре.** [tsɛ nɛ'dɔbrɛ.]
It's bad.	**Це погано.** [tsɛ po'ɦano.]
It's very bad.	**Це дуже погано.** [tsɛ 'duʒɛ po'ɦano.]
It's disgusting.	**Це огидно.** [tsɛ o'ɦidno.]

I'm happy.	**Я щасливий /щаслива/.** [ja ɕas'łiwij /ɕas'łiwa/.]
I'm content.	**Я задоволений /задоволена/.** [ja zado'wɔlɛnij /zado'wɔlɛna/.]
I'm in love.	**Я закоханий /закохана/.** [ja za'kɔhanij /za'kɔhana/.]
I'm calm.	**Я спокійний /спокійна/.** [ja spo'kijnij /spo'kijna/.]
I'm bored.	**Мені нудно.** [mɛ'ni 'nudno.]

I'm tired.	**Я втомився /втомилася/.** [ja wto'mіwsʲa /wto'mіɫasʲa/.]
I'm sad.	**Мені сумно.** [mɛ'ni 'sumno.]
I'm frightened.	**Я наляканий /налякана/.** [ja na'lʲakanij /na'lʲakana/.]

I'm angry.	**Я злюся.** [ja 'zlʲusʲa.]
I'm worried.	**Я хвилююся.** [ja hwі'lʲuʲusʲa.]
I'm nervous.	**Я нервую.** [ja nɛr'wuʲu.]

I'm jealous. (envious)

Я заздрю.
[ja 'zazdrʲu.]

I'm surprised.

Я здивований /здивована/.
[ja zdɨ'wɔwanɨj /zdɨ'wɔwana/.]

I'm perplexed.

Я спантеличений /спантеличена/.
[ja spantɛ'lɨtʃɛnɨj /spantɛ'lɨtʃɛna/.]

Problems. Accidents

I've got a problem.	**В мене проблема.** [w 'mɛnɛ prob'lɛma.]
We've got a problem.	**У нас проблема.** [u nas prob'lɛma.]
I'm lost.	**Я заблукав /заблукала/.** [ja zablu'kaw /zablu'kala/.]
I missed the last bus (train).	**Я запізнився на останній автобус (поїзд).** [ja zapiz'niwsʲa na os'tanij aw'tobus ('pɔizd).]
I don't have any money left.	**У мене зовсім не залишилося грошей.** [u 'mɛnɛ 'zɔwsim nɛ za'lɨ'ʃɨlosʲa 'ɦrɔʃɛj.]

I've lost my ...	**Я загубив /загубила/ ...** [ja zaɦu'bɨw /zaɦu'bɨla/ ...]
Someone stole my ...	**В мене вкрали ...** [w 'mɛnɛ 'wkralɨ ...]
passport	**паспорт** ['pasport]
wallet	**гаманець** [ɦama'nɛʦ]
papers	**документи** [doku'mɛntɨ]
ticket	**квиток** [kwɨ'tɔk]
money	**гроші** ['ɦrɔʃi]
handbag	**сумку** ['sumku]
camera	**фотоапарат** [fotoapa'rat]
laptop	**ноутбук** [nout'buk]
tablet computer	**планшет** [plan'ʃɛt]
mobile phone	**телефон** [tɛlɛ'fɔn]

Help me!	**Допоможіть!** [dopomo'ʒitʲ]
What's happened?	**Що трапилося?** [ɕo 'trapɨlosʲa?]

fire	**пожежа** [po'ʒɛʒa]
shooting	**стрілянина** [striʎa'nina]
murder	**вбивство** ['wbiwstwo]
explosion	**вибух** ['wibuh]
fight	**бійка** ['bijka]

Call the police!	**Викличте поліцію!** ['wiklitʃtɛ po'litsʲuǃ]
Please hurry up!	**Будь ласка, швидше!** [budʲ 'laska, 'ʃwidʃɛǃ]
I'm looking for the police station.	**Я шукаю поліцейську дільницю.** [ja ʃu'kaʲu poli'tsɛjsʲku diʎ'nitsʲu.]
I need to make a call.	**Мені треба зателефонувати.** [mɛ'ni 'trɛba zatɛlɛfonu'wati.]
May I use your phone?	**Чи можна мені зателефонувати?** [tʃi 'moʒna mɛ'ni zatɛlɛfonu'wati?]

I've been …	**Мене …** [mɛ'nɛ …]
mugged	**пограбували** [poɦrabu'wali]
robbed	**обікрали** [obi'krali]
raped	**зґвалтували** [zgwaltu'wali]
attacked (beaten up)	**побили** [po'bili]

Are you all right?	**З вами все гаразд?** [z 'wami wsɛ ɦa'razd?]
Did you see who it was?	**Ви бачили, хто це був?** [wi 'batʃili, hto tsɛ buw?]
Would you be able to recognize the person?	**Ви зможете його впізнати?** [wi 'zmoʒɛtɛ ʲo'ɦo wpiz'nati?]
Are you sure?	**Ви точно впевнені?** [wi 'totʃno 'wpɛwnɛni?]

Please calm down.	**Будь ласка, заспокойтеся.** [budʲ 'laska, zaspo'kojtɛsʲa.]
Take it easy!	**Спокійніше!** [spokij'niʃɛǃ]
Don't worry!	**Не турбуйтесь.** [nɛ tur'bujtɛsʲ.]
Everything will be fine.	**Все буде добре.** [wsɛ 'budɛ 'dobrɛ.]
Everything's all right.	**Все гаразд.** [wsɛ ɦa'razd.]

Come here, please.

Підійдіть, будь ласка.
[pidij'dit', bud' 'laska.]

I have some questions for you.

У мене до вас кілька запитань.
[u 'mɛnɛ do was 'kil'ka zapi'tanʲ.]

Wait a moment, please.

Зачекайте, будь ласка.
[zatʃɛ'kajtɛ, budʲ 'laska.]

Do you have any I.D.?

У вас є документи?
[u was 'ɛ doku'mɛnti?]

Thanks. You can leave now.

Дякую. Ви можете йти.
['dʲakuʲu. wɨ 'mɔʒɛtɛ jtɨ.]

Hands behind your head!

Руки за голову!
['rukɨ za 'hɔlowu!]

You're under arrest!

Ви заарештовані!
[wɨ zaarɛʃ'towani!]

Health problems

Please help me.	**Допоможіть, будь ласка.** [dopomo'ʒitʲ, budʲ 'laska.]
I don't feel well.	**Мені погано.** [mɛ'ni po'ɦano.]
My husband doesn't feel well.	**Моєму чоловікові погано.** [mo'ɛmu ʧolo'wikowi po'ɦano.]
My son ...	**Моєму сину ...** [mo'ɛmu 'sɨnu ...]
My father ...	**Моєму батькові ...** [mo'ɛmu 'batʲkowi ...]
My wife doesn't feel well.	**Моїй дружині погано.** [mo'ij dru'ʒini po'ɦano.]
My daughter ...	**Моїй дочці ...** [mo'ij doʧʲtsi ...]
My mother ...	**Моїй матері ...** [mo'ij 'matɛri ...]
I've got a ...	**У мене болить ...** [u 'mɛnɛ bo'litʲ ...]
headache	**голова** [ɦolo'wa]
sore throat	**горло** ['ɦɔrlo]
stomach ache	**живіт** [ʒɨ'wit]
toothache	**зуб** [zub]
I feel dizzy.	**У мене паморочиться голова.** [u 'mɛnɛ 'pamoroʧʲtsʲa ɦolo'wa.]
He has a fever.	**У нього температура.** [u 'nʲoɦo tɛmpɛra'tura.]
She has a fever.	**У неї температура.** [u nɛi tɛmpɛra'tura.]
I can't breathe.	**Я не можу дихати.** [ja nɛ 'mɔʒu 'dɨhatɨ.]
I'm short of breath.	**Я задихаюсь.** [ja zadɨ'haʲusʲ.]
I am asthmatic.	**Я астматик.** [ja ast'matɨk.]
I am diabetic.	**Я діабетик.** [ja dia'bɛtɨk.]

I can't sleep.

В мене безсоння.
[w 'mɛnɛ bɛz'sɔnʲa.]

food poisoning

харчове отруєння
[harʧo'wɛ ot'ruɛnʲa]

It hurts here.

Болить ось тут.
[bo'lʲitʲ osʲ tut.]

Help me!

Допоможіть!
[dopomo'ʒitʲ!]

I am here!

Я тут!
[ja tutʲ!]

We are here!

Ми тут!
[mʲi tutʲ!]

Get me out of here!

Витягніть мене!
['wʲitʲaɦnitʲ mɛ'nɛ!]

I need a doctor.

Мені потрібен лікар.
[mɛ'ni po'tribɛn 'likar.]

I can't move.

Я не можу рухатися.
[ja nɛ 'mɔʒu 'ruhatisʲa.]

I can't move my legs.

Я не відчуваю ніг.
[ja nɛ widʧu'waʲu niɦ.]

I have a wound.

Я поранений /поранена/.
[ja po'ranɛnij /po'ranɛna/.]

Is it serious?

Це серйозно?
[ʦɛ sɛrʲjozno?]

My documents are in my pocket.

Мої документи в кишені.
[mo'i doku'mɛnti w kiʲʃɛni.]

Calm down!

Заспокойтеся!
[zaspo'kojtɛsʲa!]

May I use your phone?

Чи можна мені зателефонувати?
[ʧʲi 'mɔʒna mɛ'ni zatɛlɛfonu'wati?]

Call an ambulance!

Викличте швидку!
['wʲiklʲiʧtɛ ʃwʲid'ku!]

It's urgent!

Це терміново!
[ʦɛ tɛrmi'nɔwo!]

It's an emergency!

Це дуже терміново!
[ʦɛ 'duʒɛ tɛrmi'nɔwo!]

Please hurry up!

Будь ласка, швидше!
[budʲ 'laska, 'ʃwʲidʃɛ!]

Would you please call a doctor?

Викличте лікаря, будь ласка.
['wʲiklʲiʧtɛ 'likarʲa, budʲ 'laska.]

Where is the hospital?

Скажіть, де лікарня?
[ska'ʒitʲ, dɛ li'karnʲa?]

How are you feeling?

Як ви себе почуваєте?
[jak wʲi sɛ'bɛ poʧu'waɛtɛ?]

Are you all right?

З вами все гаразд?
[z 'wamʲi wsɛ ɦa'razd?]

What's happened?

Що трапилося?
[ɕo 'trapʲilosʲa?]

I feel better now.	**Мені вже краще.** [mɛ'ni wʒɛ 'kraɕɛ.]
It's OK.	**Все гаразд.** [wsɛ ɦa'razd.]
It's all right.	**Все добре.** [wsɛ 'dɔbrɛ.]

At the pharmacy

pharmacy (drugstore)	**аптека** [ap'tɛka]
24-hour pharmacy	**цілодобова аптека** [ʦilodo'bowa ap'tɛka]
Where is the closest pharmacy?	**Де найближча аптека?** [dɛ najb'liʒʧa ap'tɛka?]
Is it open now?	**Вона зараз відкрита?** [wo'na 'zaraz wid'krita?]
At what time does it open?	**О котрій вона відкривається?** [o kot'rij wo'na widkriˈwaɛtsʲa?]
At what time does it close?	**До котрої години вона працює?** [do ko'trɔi ɦo'dini wo'na praˈʦʲuɛ?]
Is it far?	**Це далеко?** [ʦɛ da'lɛko?]
Can I get there on foot?	**Я дійду туди пішки?** [ja dij'du tu'di 'piʃki?]
Can you show me on the map?	**Покажіть мені на карті, будь ласка.** [poka'ʒitʲ mɛ'ni na 'karti, budʲ 'laska.]
Please give me something for ...	**Дайте мені, що-небудь від ...** ['dajtɛ mɛ'ni, ɕo-'nɛbudʲ wid ...]
a headache	**головного болю** [ɦolow'nɔɦo 'bɔlʲu]
a cough	**кашлю** ['kaʃlʲu]
a cold	**застуди** [za'studi]
the flu	**грипу** ['ɦripu]
a fever	**температури** [tɛmpɛra'turi]
a stomach ache	**болю в шлунку** ['bɔlʲu w 'ʃlunku]
nausea	**нудоти** [nu'dɔti]
diarrhea	**діареї** [dia'rɛi]
constipation	**запору** [za'pɔru]
pain in the back	**біль у спині** ['bilʲ u spi'ni]

chest pain	**біль у грудях**
	['bilʲ u 'ɦrudʲah]
side stitch	**біль у боці**
	['bilʲ u 'bɔtsi]
abdominal pain	**біль в животі**
	['bilʲ w ʒɨwo'ti]

pill	**таблетка**
	[tab'lɛtka]
ointment, cream	**мазь, крем**
	[mazʲ, krɛm]
syrup	**сироп**
	[sɨ'rɔp]
spray	**спрей**
	['sprɛj]
drops	**краплі**
	['krapli]

You need to go to the hospital.	**Вам потрібно в лікарню.**
	[wam po'tribno w li'karnʲu.]
health insurance	**страховка**
	[stra'hɔwka]
prescription	**рецепт**
	[rɛ'tsɛpt]
insect repellant	**засіб від комах**
	['zasib wid ko'mah]
Band Aid	**лейкопластир**
	[lɛjko'plastɨr]

The bare minimum

Excuse me, ...	**Вибачте, ...** ['wɨbatʃtɛ, ...]
Hello.	**Добрий день.** ['dobrɨj dɛnʲ.]
Thank you.	**Дякую.** ['dʲakuʲu.]
Good bye.	**До побачення.** [do po'batʃɛnʲa.]
Yes.	**Так.** [tak.]
No.	**Ні.** [ni.]
I don't know.	**Я не знаю.** [ja nɛ 'znaʲu.]
Where?	Where to?	When?	**Де?	Куди?	Коли?** [dɛ?	ku'dɨ?	ko'lɨ?]
I need ...	**Мені потрібен ...** [mɛ'ni po'tribɛn ...]
I want ...	**Я хочу ...** [ja 'hɔtʃu ...]
Do you have ...?	**У вас є ...?** [u was 'ɛ ...?]
Is there a ... here?	**Тут є ...?** [tut ɛ ...?]
May I ...?	**Чи можна мені ...?** [tʃɨ 'mɔʒna mɛ'ni ...?]
..., please (polite request)	**Будь ласка** [budʲ 'laska]
I'm looking for ...	**Я шукаю ...** [ja ʃu'kaʲu ...]
restroom	**туалет** [tua'lɛt]
ATM	**банкомат** [banko'mat]
pharmacy (drugstore)	**аптеку** [ap'tɛku]
hospital	**лікарню** [li'karnʲu]
police station	**поліцейську дільницю** [poli'tsɛjsʲku dilʲ'nɨtsʲu]
subway	**метро** [mɛt'rɔ]

taxi	**таксі** [tak'si]
train station	**вокзал** [wok'zal]

My name is ...	**Мене звуть ...** [mɛ'nɛ zwutʲ ...]
What's your name?	**Як вас звуть?** [jak was 'zwutʲ?]
Could you please help me?	**Допоможіть мені, будь ласка.** [dopomo'ʒitʲ mɛ'ni, budʲ 'laska.]
I've got a problem.	**У мене проблема.** [u 'mɛnɛ prob'lɛma.]
I don't feel well.	**Мені погано.** [mɛ'ni po'ɦano.]
Call an ambulance!	**Викличте швидку!** ['wiklitʃtɛ ʃwid'ku!]
May I make a call?	**Чи можна мені зателефонувати?** [tʃi 'moʒna mɛ'ni zatɛlɛfonu'watʲ?]

I'm sorry.	**Прошу вибачення** ['proʃu 'wibatʃɛnʲa]
You're welcome.	**Прошу** ['proʃu]

I, me	**я** [ja]
you (inform.)	**ти** [tɨ]
he	**він** [win]
she	**вона** [wo'na]
they (masc.)	**вони** [wo'nɨ]
they (fem.)	**вони** [wo'nɨ]
we	**ми** [mɨ]
you (pl)	**ви** [wɨ]
you (sg, form.)	**Ви** [wɨ]

ENTRANCE	**ВХІД** ['whid]
EXIT	**ВИХІД** ['wihid]
OUT OF ORDER	**НЕ ПРАЦЮЄ** [nɛ pra'tsʲuɛ]
CLOSED	**ЗАКРИТО** [za'krito]

OPEN

ВІДКРИТО
[wid'krito]

FOR WOMEN

ДЛЯ ЖІНОК
[dlʲa ʒi'nɔk]

FOR MEN

ДЛЯ ЧОЛОВІКІВ
[dlʲa ʧolowi'kiw]

CONCISE DICTIONARY

This section contains more than 1,500 useful words arranged alphabetically. The dictionary includes a lot of gastronomic terms and will be helpful when ordering food at a restaurant or buying groceries

T&P Books Publishing

DICTIONARY CONTENTS

T&P Books Publishing

time	час (с)	[ʧas]
hour	година (ж)	[ɦoˈdɨna]
half an hour	півгодини (мн)	[piwɦoˈdɨnɨ]
minute	хвилина (ж)	[hwɨˈlina]
second	секунда (ж)	[sɛˈkunda]
today (adv)	сьогодні	[sʲoˈɦɔdni]
tomorrow (adv)	завтра	[ˈzawtra]
yesterday (adv)	вчора	[ˈwʧɔra]
Monday	понеділок (ч)	[ponɛˈdilok]
Tuesday	вівторок (ч)	[wiwˈtɔrok]
Wednesday	середа (ж)	[sɛrɛˈda]
Thursday	четвер (ч)	[ʧɛtˈwɛr]
Friday	п'ятниця (ж)	[ˈpʲatnɨtsʲa]
Saturday	субота (ж)	[suˈbɔta]
Sunday	неділя (ж)	[nɛˈdilʲa]
day	день (ч)	[dɛnʲ]
working day	робочий день (ч)	[roˈbɔʧɨj dɛnʲ]
public holiday	святковий день (ч)	[swʲatˈkɔwɨj dɛnʲ]
weekend	вихідні (мн)	[wɨhidˈni]
week	тиждень (ч)	[ˈtɨʒdɛnʲ]
last week (adv)	на минулому тижні	[na mɨˈnulomu ˈtɨʒni]
next week (adv)	на наступному тижні	[na naˈstupnomu ˈtɨʒni]
sunrise	схід (ч) сонця	[shid ˈsɔntsʲa]
sunset	захід (ч)	[ˈzahid]
in the morning	вранці	[ˈwrantsi]
in the afternoon	після обіду	[ˈpislʲa oˈbidu]
in the evening	увечері	[uˈwɛʧɛri]
tonight (this evening)	сьогодні увечері	[sʲoˈɦɔdni uˈwɛʧɛri]
at night	уночі	[unoˈʧi]
midnight	північ (ж)	[ˈpiwniʧ]
January	січень (ч)	[ˈsiʧɛnʲ]
February	лютий (ч)	[ˈlʲutɨj]
March	березень (ч)	[ˈbɛrɛzɛnʲ]
April	квітень (ч)	[ˈkwitɛnʲ]
May	травень (ч)	[ˈtrawɛnʲ]
June	червень (ч)	[ˈʧɛrwɛnʲ]

July	липень (ч)	['łipɛnʲ]
August	серпень (ч)	['sɛrpɛnʲ]
September	вересень (ч)	['wɛrɛsɛnʲ]
October	жовтень (ч)	['ʒowtɛnʲ]
November	листопад (ч)	[łisto'pad]
December	грудень (ч)	['ɦrudɛnʲ]

in spring	навесні	[nawɛs'ni]
in summer	влітку	['wlitku]
in fall	восени	[wosɛ'nɨ]
in winter	взимку	['wzɨmku]

month	місяць (ч)	['misʲaʦ]
season (summer, etc.)	сезон (ч)	[sɛ'zɔn]
year	рік (ч)	[rik]
century	вік (ч)	[wik]

2. Numbers. Numerals

digit, figure	цифра (ж)	['ʦɨfra]
number	число (с)	[ʧɨs'łɔ]
minus sign	мінус (ч)	['minus]
plus sign	плюс (ч)	[plʲus]
sum, total	сума (ж)	['suma]

first (adj)	перший	['pɛrʃɨj]
second (adj)	другий	['druɦɨj]
third (adj)	третій	['trɛtij]

0 zero	нуль	[nulʲ]
1 one	один	[o'dɨn]
2 two	два	[dwa]
3 three	три	[trɨ]
4 four	чотири	[ʧo'tɨrɨ]

5 five	п'ять	[pʲatʲ]
6 six	шість	[ʃistʲ]
7 seven	сім	[sim]
8 eight	вісім	['wisim]
9 nine	дев'ять	['dɛwʲatʲ]
10 ten	десять	['dɛsʲatʲ]

11 eleven	одинадцять	[odɨ'nadʦʲatʲ]
12 twelve	дванадцять	[dwa'nadʦʲatʲ]
13 thirteen	тринадцять	[trɨ'nadʦʲatʲ]
14 fourteen	чотирнадцять	[ʧotɨr'nadʦʲatʲ]
15 fifteen	п'ятнадцять	[pʲat'nadʦʲatʲ]

16 sixteen	шістнадцять	[ʃist'nadʦʲatʲ]
17 seventeen	сімнадцять	[sim'nadʦʲatʲ]

| 18 eighteen | вісімнадцять | [wisim'nadtsʲatʲ] |
| 19 nineteen | дев'ятнадцять | [dɛwʲat'nadtsʲatʲ] |

20 twenty	двадцять	['dwadtsʲatʲ]
30 thirty	тридцять	['tridtsʲatʲ]
40 forty	сорок	['sɔrok]
50 fifty	п'ятдесят	[pʲatdɛ'sʲat]

60 sixty	шістдесят	[ʃizdɛ'sʲat]
70 seventy	сімдесят	[simdɛ'sʲat]
80 eighty	вісімдесят	[wisimdɛ'sʲat]
90 ninety	дев'яносто	[dɛwʲa'nɔsto]

100 one hundred	сто	[sto]
200 two hundred	двісті	['dwisti]
300 three hundred	триста	['trista]
400 four hundred	чотириста	[tʃo'tirista]
500 five hundred	п'ятсот	[pʲa'tsɔt]

600 six hundred	шістсот	[ʃist'sɔt]
700 seven hundred	сімсот	[sim'sɔt]
800 eight hundred	вісімсот	[wisim'sɔt]
900 nine hundred	дев'ятсот	[dɛwʲa'tsɔt]
1000 one thousand	тисяча	['tisʲatʃa]

| 10000 ten thousand | десять тисяч | ['dɛsʲatʲ 'tisʲatʃ] |
| one hundred thousand | сто тисяч | [sto 'tisʲatʃ] |

| million | мільйон (ч) | [milʲ'jon] |
| billion | мільярд (ч) | [mi'ljard] |

3. Humans. Family

man (adult male)	чоловік (ч)	[tʃolo'wik]
young man	юнак (ч)	[ʲu'nak]
teenager	підліток (ч)	['pidlitok]
woman	жінка (ж)	['ʒinka]
girl (young woman)	дівчина (ж)	['diwtʃina]

age	вік (ч)	[wik]
adult (adj)	дорослий	[do'rɔslij]
middle-aged (adj)	середніх років	[sɛ'rɛdnih ro'kiw]
elderly (adj)	похилий	[po'hiłij]
old (adj)	старий	[sta'rij]

old man	старий (ч)	[sta'rij]
old woman	стара (ж)	[sta'ra]
retirement	пенсія (ж)	['pɛnsʲia]
to retire (from job)	вийти на пенсію	['wijti na 'pɛnsʲʲu]
retiree	пенсіонер (ч)	[pɛnsio'nɛr]

mother	мати (ж)	['mati]
father	батько (ч)	['batʲko]
son	син (ч)	[sɨn]
daughter	дочка (ж)	[dotʃˈka]
brother	брат (ч)	[brat]
sister	сестра (ж)	[sɛstˈra]

parents	батьки (мн)	[batʲˈkɨ]
child	дитина (ж)	[dɨˈtɨna]
children	діти (мн)	['ditɨ]
stepmother	мачуха (ж)	['matʃuha]
stepfather	вітчим (ч)	['witʃɨm]

grandmother	бабуся (ж)	[baˈbusʲa]
grandfather	дід (ч)	['did]
grandson	онук (ч)	[oˈnuk]
granddaughter	онука (ж)	[oˈnuka]
grandchildren	онуки (мн)	[oˈnukɨ]

uncle	дядько (ч)	['dʲadʲko]
aunt	тітка (ж)	['titka]
nephew	племінник (ч)	[plɛˈminɨk]
niece	племінниця (ж)	[plɛˈminɨtsʲa]

wife	дружина (ж)	[druˈʒɨna]
husband	чоловік (ч)	[tʃoloˈwik]
married (masc.)	одружений	[odˈruʒɛnɨj]
married (fem.)	заміжня	[zaˈmiʒnʲa]
widow	вдова (ж)	[wdoˈwa]
widower	вдівець (ч)	[wdiˈwɛts]

| name (first name) | ім'я (с) | [iˈmʲ˞a] |
| surname (last name) | прізвище (с) | ['prizwɨɕɛ] |

relative	родич (ч)	['rɔdɨtʃ]
friend (masc.)	товариш (ч)	[toˈwarɨʃ]
friendship	дружба (ж)	['druʒba]

partner	партнер (ч)	[partˈnɛr]
superior (n)	начальник (ч)	[naˈtʃalʲnɨk]
colleague	колега (ч)	[koˈlɛɦa]
neighbors	сусіди (мн)	[suˈsidɨ]

4. Human body

organism (body)	організм (ч)	[orɦaˈnizm]
body	тіло (с)	['tilo]
heart	серце (с)	['sɛrtsɛ]
blood	кров (ж)	[krow]
brain	мозок (ч)	['mɔzok]

nerve	нерв (ч)	[nɛrw]
bone	кістка (ж)	['kistka]
skeleton	скелет (ч)	[skɛ'lɛt]
spine (backbone)	хребет (ч)	[hrɛ'bɛt]
rib	ребро (с)	[rɛb'rɔ]
skull	череп (ч)	['ʧɛrɛp]

muscle	м'яз (ч)	['mʲaz]
lungs	легені (мн)	[lɛ'hɛni]
skin	шкіра (ж)	['ʃkira]

head	голова (ж)	[ɦolo'wa]
face	обличчя (с)	[ob'liʧʲa]
nose	ніс (ч)	[nis]
forehead	чоло (с)	[ʧo'lɔ]
cheek	щока (ж)	[ɕo'ka]

mouth	рот (ч)	[rot]
tongue	язик (ч)	[ja'zik]
tooth	зуб (ч)	[zub]
lips	губи (мн)	['ɦubi]
chin	підборіддя (с)	[pidbo'riddʲa]

ear	вухо (с)	['wuɦo]
neck	шия (ж)	['ʃiʲa]
throat	горло (с)	['ɦɔrlo]

eye	око (с)	['ɔko]
pupil	зіниця (ч)	[zi'nitsʲa]
eyebrow	брова (ж)	[bro'wa]
eyelash	вія (ж)	['wiʲa]

hair	волосся (с)	[wo'lɔssʲa]
hairstyle	зачіска (ж)	['zaʧiska]
mustache	вуса (мн)	['wusa]
beard	борода (ж)	[boro'da]
to have (a beard, etc.)	носити	[no'siti]
bald (adj)	лисий	['lisij]

hand	кисть (ж)	[kistʲ]
arm	рука (ж)	[ru'ka]
finger	палець (ч)	['palɛts]
nail	ніготь (ч)	['niɦotʲ]
palm	долоня (ж)	[do'lɔnʲa]

shoulder	плече (с)	[plɛ'ʧɛ]
leg	гомілка (ж)	[ɦo'milka]
foot	ступня (ж)	[stup'nʲa]
knee	коліно (с)	[ko'lino]
heel	п'ятка (ж)	['pʲatka]
back	спина (ж)	['spina]
waist	талія (ж)	['taliʲa]

| beauty mark | родимка (ж) | ['rɔdɨmka] |
| birthmark (café au lait spot) | родима пляма (ж) | [ro'dɨma 'plʲama] |

5. Medicine. Diseases. Drugs

health	здоров'я (с)	[zdo'rɔwˀʲa]
well (not sick)	здоровий	[zdo'rɔwɨj]
sickness	хвороба (ж)	[hwo'rɔba]
to be sick	хворіти	[hwo'ritɨ]
ill, sick (adj)	хворий	['hwɔrɨj]

cold (illness)	застуда (ж)	[za'studa]
to catch a cold	застудитися	[zastu'dɨtɨsʲa]
tonsillitis	ангіна (ж)	[an'hina]
pneumonia	запалення (с) легенів	[za'palɛnja lɛ'hɛniw]
flu, influenza	грип (ч)	[hrɨp]

runny nose (coryza)	нежить (ч)	['nɛʒɨtʲ]
cough	кашель (ч)	['kaʃɛlʲ]
to cough (vi)	кашляти	['kaʃlʲatɨ]
to sneeze (vi)	чхати	['ʧhatɨ]

stroke	інсульт (ч)	[in'sulʲt]
heart attack	інфаркт (ч)	[in'farkt]
allergy	алергія (ж)	[alɛr'hiʲa]
asthma	астма (ж)	['astma]
diabetes	діабет (ч)	[dia'bɛt]

tumor	пухлина (ж)	[puh'lɨna]
cancer	рак (ч)	[rak]
alcoholism	алкоголізм (ч)	[alkoho'lizm]
AIDS	СНІД (ч)	[snid]
fever	гарячка (ж)	[ha'rʲatʃka]
seasickness	морська хвороба (ж)	[morsʲ'ka hwo'rɔba]

bruise (hématome)	синець (ч)	[sɨ'nɛʦ]
bump (lump)	гуля (ж)	['hulʲa]
to limp (vi)	кульгати	[kulʲ'hatɨ]
dislocation	вивих (ч)	['wɨwɨh]
to dislocate (vt)	вивихнути	['wɨwɨhnutɨ]

fracture	перелом (ч)	[pɛrɛ'lɔm]
burn (injury)	опік (ч)	['ɔpik]
injury	ушкодження (с)	[uʃ'kɔdʒɛnʲa]
pain, ache	біль (ч)	[bilʲ]
toothache	зубний біль (ч)	[zub'nɨj bilʲ]

| to sweat (perspire) | спітніти | [spit'nitɨ] |
| deaf (adj) | глухий (ч) | [hlu'hɨj] |

mute (adj)	німий (ч)	[ni'mij]
immunity	імунітет (ч)	[imuni'tɛt]
virus	вірус (ч)	['wirus]
microbe	мікроб (ч)	[mik'rɔb]
bacterium	бактерія (ж)	[bak'tɛriˈa]
infection	інфекція (ж)	[in'fɛktsiˈa]

hospital	лікарня (ж)	[liˈkarnˈa]
cure	лікування (с)	[liku'wanˈa]
to vaccinate (vt)	робити щеплення	[ro'biti 'ɕɛplɛnˈa]
to be in a coma	бути в комі	['buti w 'kɔmi]
intensive care	реанімація (ж)	[rɛani'matsiˈa]
symptom	симптом (ч)	[sɨmp'tɔm]
pulse	пульс (ч)	[pulˈs]

6. Feelings. Emotions. Conversation

I, me	я	[ja]
you	ти	[tɨ]
he	він	[win]
she	вона	[wo'na]

we	ми	[mɨ]
you (to a group)	ви	[wɨ]
they	вони	[wo'nɨ]

Hello! (fam.)	Здрастуй!	['zdrastuj]
Hello! (form.)	Здрастуйте!	['zdrastujtɛ]
Good morning!	Доброго ранку!	['dɔbrofo 'ranku]
Good afternoon!	Добрий день!	['dɔbrij dɛnˈ]
Good evening!	Добрий вечір!	['dɔbrij 'wɛtʃir]

to say hello	вітатися	[wi'tatisˈa]
to greet (vt)	вітати	[wi'tati]
How are you?	Як справи?	[jak 'sprawɨ]
Bye-Bye! Goodbye!	До побачення!	[do po'batʃɛnˈa]
Thank you!	Дякую!	['dˈakuˈu]

feelings	почуття (мн)	[potʃutˈtˈa]
to be hungry	хотіти їсти	[ho'titi 'jisti]
to be thirsty	хотіти пити	[ho'titi 'pɨti]
tired (adj)	втомлений	['wtɔmlɛnij]

to be worried	хвилюватися	[hwilˈu'watisˈa]
to be nervous	нервуватися	[nɛrwu'watisˈa]
hope	надія (ж)	[na'diˈa]
to hope (vi, vt)	сподіватися	[spodi'watisˈa]

| character | характер (ч) | [ha'raktɛr] |
| modest (adj) | скромний | ['skrɔmnij] |

lazy (adj)	ледачий	[lɛ'datʃij]
generous (adj)	щедрий	['ɕɛdrij]
talented (adj)	талановитий	[talano'wіtіj]

honest (adj)	чесний	['tʃɛsnіj]
serious (adj)	серйозний	[sɛrʲoznіj]
shy, timid (adj)	сором'язливий	[soro'mʲazlіwіj]
sincere (adj)	щирий	['ɕіrіj]
coward	боягуз (ч)	[boja'ɦuz]

to sleep (vi)	спати	['spatі]
dream	сон (ч)	[son]
bed	ліжко (с)	['liʒko]
pillow	подушка (ж)	[po'duʃka]

insomnia	безсоння (с)	[bɛz'sonʲa]
to go to bed	йти спати	[jtі 'spatі]
nightmare	страхіття (с)	[stra'hіttʲa]
alarm clock	будильник (ч)	[bu'dіlʲnіk]

smile	посмішка (ж)	['pɔsmiʃka]
to smile (vi)	посміхатися	[posmi'hatisʲa]
to laugh (vi)	сміятися	[smiʲ'atisʲa]

quarrel	сварка (ж)	['swarka]
insult	образа (ж)	[ob'raza]
resentment	образа (ж)	[ob'raza]
angry (mad)	сердитий	[sɛr'dіtіj]

7. Clothing. Personal accessories

clothes	одяг (ч)	['ɔdʲaɦ]
coat (overcoat)	пальто (с)	[palʲ'to]
fur coat	шуба (ж)	['ʃuba]
jacket (e.g., leather ~)	куртка (ж)	['kurtka]
raincoat (trenchcoat, etc.)	плащ (ч)	[plaɕ]

shirt (button shirt)	сорочка (ж)	[so'rɔtʃka]
pants	штани (мн)	[ʃta'nі]
suit jacket	піджак (ч)	[pi'dʒak]
suit	костюм (ч)	[kos'tʲum]

dress (frock)	сукня (ж)	['suknʲa]
skirt	спідниця (ж)	[spid'nіtsʲa]
T-shirt	футболка (ж)	[fut'bɔlka]
bathrobe	халат (ч)	[ha'lat]
pajamas	піжама (ж)	[pi'ʒama]
workwear	робочий одяг (ж)	[ro'bɔtʃij 'ɔdʲaɦ]
underwear	білизна (ж)	[bi'lіzna]
socks	шкарпетки (мн)	[ʃkar'pɛtkі]

bra	бюстгальтер (ч)	[bʲust'halʲtɛr]
pantyhose	колготки (мн)	[kol'hɔtki]
stockings (thigh highs)	панчохи (мн)	[pan'tʃɔhi]
bathing suit	купальник (ч)	[ku'palʲnik]
hat	шапка (ж)	['ʃapka]
footwear	взуття (с)	[wzut'tʲa]
boots (e.g., cowboy ~)	чоботи (мн)	['tʃɔboti]
heel	каблук (ч)	[kab'luk]
shoestring	шнурок (ч)	[ʃnu'rɔk]
shoe polish	крем (ч) для взуття	[krɛm dlʲa wzut'tʲa]
cotton (n)	бавовна (ж)	[ba'wɔwna]
wool (n)	вовна (ж)	['wɔwna]
fur (n)	хутро (с)	['hutro]
gloves	рукавички (мн)	[ruka'witʃki]
mittens	рукавиці (мн)	[ruka'witsi]
scarf (muffler)	шарф (ч)	[ʃarf]
glasses (eyeglasses)	окуляри (мн)	[oku'lʲari]
umbrella	парасолька (ж)	[para'sɔlʲka]
tie (necktie)	краватка (ж)	[kra'watka]
handkerchief	носовичок (ч)	[nosowi'tʃɔk]
comb	гребінець (ч)	[ɦrɛbi'nɛts]
hairbrush	щітка (ж) для волосся	['ɕitka dlʲa wo'lɔssʲa]
buckle	пряжка (ж)	['prʲaʒka]
belt	пасок (ч)	['pasok]
purse	сумочка (ж)	['sumotʃka]
collar	комір (ч)	['kɔmir]
pocket	кишеня (ж)	[ki'ʃɛnʲa]
sleeve	рукав (ч)	[ru'kaw]
fly (on trousers)	ширінка (ж)	[ʃʲi'rinka]
zipper (fastener)	змійка (ж)	['zmijka]
button	ґудзик (ч)	['gudzik]
to get dirty (vi)	забруднитися	[zabrud'nitisʲa]
stain (mark, spot)	пляма (ж)	['plʲama]

8. City. Urban institutions

store	магазин (ч)	[maɦa'zin]
shopping mall	торгівельний центр (ч)	[torɦi'wɛlʲnij 'tsɛntr]
supermarket	супермаркет (ч)	[supɛr'markɛt]
shoe store	взуттєвий магазин (ч)	[wzut'tɛwij maɦa'zin]
bookstore	книгарня (ж)	[kni'ɦarnʲa]
drugstore, pharmacy	аптека (ж)	[ap'tɛka]
bakery	булочна (ж)	['bulotʃna]

pastry shop	кондитерська (ж)	[kon'ditɛrsʲka]
grocery store	бакалія (ж)	[baka'liʲa]
butcher shop	м'ясний магазин (ч)	[mʲas'nij maɦa'zin]
produce store	овочевий магазин (ч)	[owo'tʃɛwij maɦa'zin]
market	ринок (ч)	['rinok]

hair salon	перукарня (ж)	[pɛru'karnʲa]
post office	пошта (ж)	['poʃta]
dry cleaners	хімчистка (ж)	[him'tʃistka]
circus	цирк (ч)	[tsirk]
zoo	зоопарк (ч)	[zoo'park]

theater	театр (ч)	[tɛ'atr]
movie theater	кінотеатр (ч)	[kinotɛ'atr]
museum	музей (ч)	[mu'zɛj]
library	бібліотека (ж)	[biblio'tɛka]

mosque	мечеть (ж)	[mɛ'tʃɛtʲ]
synagogue	синагога (ж)	[sina'ɦoɦa]
cathedral	собор (ч)	[so'bor]
temple	храм (ч)	[hram]
church	церква (ж)	['tsɛrkwa]

college	інститут (ч)	[insti'tut]
university	університет (ч)	[uniwɛrsi'tɛt]
school	школа (ж)	['ʃkola]

hotel	готель (ч)	[ɦo'tɛlʲ]
bank	банк (ч)	[bank]
embassy	посольство (с)	[po'solʲstwo]
travel agency	турагентство (с)	[tura'ɦɛntstwo]

subway	метро (с)	[mɛt'ro]
hospital	лікарня (ж)	[li'karnʲa]
gas station	бензоколонка (ж)	[bɛnzoko'lonka]
parking lot	стоянка (ж)	[sto'ʲanka]

ENTRANCE	ВХІД	[whid]
EXIT	ВИХІД	['wihid]
PUSH	ВІД СЕБЕ	[wid 'sɛbɛ]
PULL	ДО СЕБЕ	[do 'sɛbɛ]
OPEN	ВІДЧИНЕНО	[wid'tʃinɛno]
CLOSED	ЗАЧИНЕНО	[za'tʃinɛno]

monument	пам'ятник (ч)	['pamʲatnik]
fortress	фортеця (ж)	[for'tɛtsʲa]
palace	палац (ч)	[pa'lats]

medieval (adj)	середньовічний	[sɛrɛdnʲo'witʃnij]
ancient (adj)	старовинний	[staro'winij]
national (adj)	національний	[natsio'nalʲnij]
famous (monument, etc.)	відомий	[wi'domij]

9. Money. Finances

money	гроші (мн)	['ɦrɔʃi]
coin	монета (ж)	[mo'nɛta]
dollar	долар (ч)	['dɔlar]
euro	євро (ч)	['ɛwro]
ATM	банкомат (ч)	[banko'mat]
currency exchange	обмінний пункт (ч)	[ob'minij punkt]
exchange rate	курс (ч)	[kurs]
cash	готівка (ж)	[ɦo'tiwka]
How much?	Скільки?	['skilʲki]
to pay (vi, vt)	платити	[pla'titi]
payment	оплата (ж)	[op'lata]
change (give the ~)	решта (ж)	['rɛʃta]
price	ціна (ж)	[ʦi'na]
discount	знижка (ж)	['zniʒka]
cheap (adj)	дешевий	[dɛ'ʃewij]
expensive (adj)	дорогий	[doro'ɦij]
bank	банк (ч)	[bank]
account	рахунок (ч)	[ra'ɦunok]
credit card	кредитна картка (ж)	[krɛ'ditna 'kartka]
check	чек (ч)	[ʧɛk]
to write a check	виписати чек	['wipisati 'ʧɛk]
checkbook	чекова книжка (ж)	['ʧɛkowa 'kniʒka]
debt	борг (ч)	['bɔrɦ]
debtor	боржник (ч)	[borʒ'nik]
to lend (money)	позичити	[po'ziʧiti]
to borrow (vi, vt)	взяти в борг	['wzʲati w borɦ]
to rent (~ a tuxedo)	взяти напрокат	['wzʲati napro'kat]
on credit (adv)	в кредит (ч)	[w krɛ'dit]
wallet	гаманець (ч)	[hama'nɛʦ]
safe	сейф (ч)	[sɛjf]
inheritance	спадщина (с)	['spadɕina]
fortune (wealth)	статок (ч)	['statok]
tax	податок (ч)	[po'datok]
fine	штраф (ч)	[ʃtraf]
to fine (vt)	штрафувати	[ʃtrafu'wati]
wholesale (adj)	оптовий	[op'tɔwij]
retail (adj)	роздрібний	[rozd'ribnij]
to insure (vt)	страхувати	[strahu'wati]
insurance	страхування (с)	[strahu'wanʲa]
capital	капітал (ч)	[kapi'tal]
turnover	обіг (ч)	['ɔbiɦ]

stock (share)	акція (ж)	['aktsiʲa]
profit	прибуток (ч)	[priˈbutok]
profitable (adj)	прибутковий	[pributˈkowij]

crisis	криза (ж)	[ˈkriza]
bankruptcy	банкрутство (с)	[banˈkrutstwo]
to go bankrupt	збанкрутувати	[zbankrutuˈwati]

accountant	бухгалтер (ч)	[buhˈhaltɛr]
salary	заробітна платня (ж)	[zaroˈbitna platˈnʲa]
bonus (money)	премія (ж)	[ˈprɛmiʲa]

10. Transportation

bus	автобус (ч)	[awˈtobus]
streetcar	трамвай (ч)	[tramˈwaj]
trolley bus	тролейбус (ч)	[troˈlɛjbus]

to go by ...	їхати на ...	[ˈjihatɨ na]
to get on (~ the bus)	сісти	[ˈsistɨ]
to get off ...	зійти	[zijˈti]

stop (e.g., bus ~)	зупинка (ж)	[zuˈpɨnka]
terminus	кінцева зупинка (ж)	[kinˈtsɛwa zuˈpɨnka]
schedule	розклад (ч)	[ˈrozklad]
ticket	квиток (ч)	[kwiˈtok]
to be late (for ...)	запізнюватися	[zaˈpiznʲuwatɨsʲa]

taxi, cab	таксі (с)	[takˈsi]
by taxi	на таксі	[na takˈsi]
taxi stand	стоянка (с) таксі	[stoˈʲanka takˈsi]

traffic	вуличний рух (ч)	[ˈwulitʃnij ruh]
rush hour	години (мн) пік	[ɦoˈdɨnɨ pik]
to park (vi)	паркуватися	[parkuˈwatisʲa]

subway	метро (с)	[mɛtˈro]
station	станція (ж)	[ˈstantsiʲa]
train	поїзд (ч)	[ˈpojizd]
train station	вокзал (ч)	[wokˈzal]
rails	рейки (мн)	[ˈrɛjkɨ]
compartment	купе (с)	[kuˈpɛ]
berth	полиця (ж)	[poˈlitsʲa]

airplane	літак (ч)	[liˈtak]
air ticket	авіаквиток (ч)	[awiakwiˈtok]
airline	авіакомпанія (ж)	[awiakomˈpaniʲa]
airport	аеропорт (ч)	[aɛroˈport]
flight (act of flying)	політ (ч)	[poˈlit]
luggage	багаж (ч)	[baˈɦaʒ]

luggage cart	візок (ч) для багажу	[wi'zɔk dlʲa baɦa'ʒu]
ship	корабель (ч)	[kora'bɛlʲ]
cruise ship	лайнер (ч)	['lajnɛr]
yacht	яхта (ж)	['ʲahta]
boat (flat-bottomed ~)	човен (ч)	['tʃowɛn]
captain	капітан (ч)	[kapi'tan]
cabin	каюта (ж)	[ka'ʲuta]
port (harbor)	порт (ч)	[port]
bicycle	велосипед (ч)	[wɛlosi'pɛd]
scooter	моторолер (ч)	[moto'rɔlɛr]
motorcycle, bike	мотоцикл (ч)	[moto'tsikl]
pedal	педаль (ж)	[pɛ'dalʲ]
pump	помпа (ж)	['pɔmpa]
wheel	колесо (с)	['kɔlɛso]
automobile, car	автомобіль (ч)	[awtomo'bilʲ]
ambulance	швидка допомога (ж)	[ʃwid'ka dopo'mɔɦa]
truck	вантажівка (ж)	[wanta'ʒiwka]
used (adj)	вживаний	['wʒiwanij]
car crash	аварія (ж)	[a'wariʲa]
repair	ремонт (ч)	[rɛ'mɔnt]

11. Food. Part 1

meat	м'ясо (с)	['mʲʲaso]
chicken	курка (ж)	['kurka]
duck	качка (ж)	['katʃka]
pork	свинина (ж)	[swi'nina]
veal	телятина (ж)	[tɛ'lʲatina]
lamb	баранина (ж)	[ba'ranina]
beef	яловичина (ж)	['ʲalowitʃina]
sausage (bologna, pepperoni, etc.)	ковбаса (ж)	[kowba'sa]
egg	яйце (с)	[jaj'tsɛ]
fish	риба (ж)	['riba]
cheese	сир (ч)	[sir]
sugar	цукор (ч)	['tsukor]
salt	сіль (ж)	[silʲ]
rice	рис (ч)	[ris]
pasta (macaroni)	макарони (мн)	[maka'rɔni]
butter	вершкове масло (с)	[wɛrʃ'kɔwɛ 'maslo]
vegetable oil	олія (ж) рослинна	[o'liʲa ros'lina]
bread	хліб (ч)	[hlib]
chocolate (n)	шоколад (ч)	[ʃoko'lad]
wine	вино (с)	[wi'nɔ]

coffee	кава (ж)	['kawa]
milk	молоко (с)	[molo'kɔ]
juice	сік (ч)	[sik]
beer	пиво (с)	['pɨwo]
tea	чай (ч)	[ʧaj]

tomato	помідор (ч)	[pomi'dɔr]
cucumber	огірок (ч)	[ohi'rɔk]
carrot	морква (ж)	['mɔrkwa]
potato	картопля (ж)	[kar'tɔplʲa]
onion	цибуля (ж)	[ʦɨ'bulʲa]
garlic	часник (ч)	[ʧas'nɨk]

cabbage	капуста (ж)	[ka'pusta]
beetroot	буряк (ч)	[bu'rʲak]
eggplant	баклажан (ч)	[bakla'ʒan]
dill	кріп (ч)	[krip]
lettuce	салат (ч)	[sa'lat]
corn (maize)	кукурудза (ж)	[kuku'ruʣa]

fruit	фрукт (ч)	[frukt]
apple	яблуко (с)	['ʲabluko]
pear	груша (ж)	['ɦruʃa]
lemon	лимон (ч)	[lɨ'mɔn]
orange	апельсин (ч)	[apɛlʲ'sɨn]
strawberry (garden ~)	полуниця (ж)	[polu'nɨʦʲa]

plum	слива (ж)	['slɨwa]
raspberry	малина (ж)	[ma'lɨna]
pineapple	ананас (ч)	[ana'nas]
banana	банан (ч)	[ba'nan]
watermelon	кавун (ч)	[ka'wun]
grape	виноград (ч)	[wɨno'ɦrad]
melon	диня (ж)	['dɨnʲa]

12. Food. Part 2

cuisine	кухня (ж)	['kuhnʲa]
recipe	рецепт (ч)	[rɛ'ʦɛpt]
food	їжа (ж)	['jiʒa]

to have breakfast	снідати	['snidatɨ]
to have lunch	обідати	[o'bidatɨ]
to have dinner	вечеряти	[wɛ'ʧɛrʲatɨ]

taste, flavor	смак (ч)	[smak]
tasty (adj)	смачний	[smaʧ'nɨj]
cold (adj)	холодний	[ho'lɔdnɨj]
hot (adj)	гарячий	[ɦa'rʲaʧɨj]
sweet (sugary)	солодкий	[so'lɔdkɨj]

salty (adj)	солоний	[so'lonij]
sandwich (bread)	канапка (ж)	[ka'napka]
side dish	гарнір (ч)	[ɦar'nir]
filling (for cake, pie)	начинка (ж)	[na'tʃinka]
sauce	соус (ч)	['sɔus]
piece (of cake, pie)	шматок (ч)	[ʃma'tɔk]

diet	дієта (ж)	[di'ɛta]
vitamin	вітамін (ч)	[wita'min]
calorie	калорія (ж)	[ka'lori͡a]
vegetarian (n)	вегетаріанець (ч)	[wɛɦɛtari'anɛts]

restaurant	ресторан (ч)	[rɛsto'ran]
coffee house	кав'ярня (ж)	[ka'w͡ʲarn͡ʲa]
appetite	апетит (ч)	[apɛ'tit]
Enjoy your meal!	Смачного!	[smatʃ'noɦo]

waiter	офіціант (ч)	[ofitsi'ant]
waitress	офіціантка (ж)	[ofitsi'antka]
bartender	бармен (ч)	[bar'mɛn]
menu	меню (с)	[mɛ'n͡ʲu]

spoon	ложка (ж)	['lɔʒka]
knife	ніж (ч)	[niʒ]
fork	виделка (ж)	[wi'dɛlka]
cup (e.g., coffee ~)	чашка (ж)	['tʃaʃka]
plate (dinner ~)	тарілка (ж)	[ta'rilka]
saucer	блюдце (с)	['bl͡ʲudtsɛ]
napkin (on table)	серветка (ж)	[sɛr'wɛtka]
toothpick	зубочистка (ж)	[zubo'tʃistka]

to order (meal)	замовити	[za'mɔwiti]
course, dish	страва (ж)	['strawa]
portion	порція (ж)	['portsi͡a]
appetizer	закуска (ж)	[za'kuska]
salad	салат (ч)	[sa'lat]
soup	юшка (ж)	['͡ʲuʃka]

dessert	десерт (ч)	[dɛ'sɛrt]
jam (whole fruit jam)	варення (с)	[wa'rɛn͡ʲa]
ice-cream	морозиво (с)	[mo'rɔziwo]

check	рахунок (ч)	[ra'ɦunok]
to pay the check	оплатити рахунок	[opla'titi ra'ɦunok]
tip	чайові (мн)	[tʃa͡ʲo'wi]

13. House. Apartment. Part 1

| house | будинок (ч) | [bu'dinok] |
| country house | будинок (ч) за містом | [bu'dinok za 'mistom] |

villa (seaside ~)	вілла (ж)	['willa]
floor, story	поверх (ч)	['pɔwɛrh]
entrance	під'їзд (ч)	[pid"jizd]
wall	стіна (ж)	[sti'na]
roof	дах (ч)	[dah]
chimney	труба (ж)	[tru'ba]
attic (storage place)	горище (с)	[ɦo'riɕɛ]
window	вікно (с)	[wik'nɔ]
window ledge	підвіконня (с)	[pidwi'kɔnʲa]
balcony	балкон (ч)	[bal'kɔn]
stairs (stairway)	сходи (мн)	['shɔdi]
mailbox	поштова скринька (ж)	[poʃ'towa sk'rinʲka]
garbage can	бак (ч) для сміття	[bak dlʲa smit'tʲa]
elevator	ліфт (ч)	[lift]
electricity	електрика (ж)	[ɛ'lɛktrika]
light bulb	лампочка (ж)	['lampoʧka]
switch	вимикач (ч)	[wimi'kaʧ]
wall socket	розетка (ж)	[ro'zɛtka]
fuse	запобіжник (ч)	[zapo'biʒnik]
door	двері (мн)	['dwɛri]
handle, doorknob	ручка (ж)	['ruʧka]
key	ключ (ч)	[klʲuʧ]
doormat	килимок (ч)	[kili'mɔk]
door lock	замок (ч)	[za'mɔk]
doorbell	дзвінок (ч)	[dzwi'nɔk]
knock (at the door)	стукіт (ч)	['stukit]
to knock (vi)	стукати	['stukati]
peephole	вічко (с)	['wiʧko]
yard	двір (ч)	[dwir]
garden	сад (ч)	[sad]
swimming pool	басейн (ч)	[ba'sɛjn]
gym (home gym)	спортивний зал (ч)	[spor'tiwnij 'zal]
tennis court	тенісний корт (ч)	['tɛnisnij 'kɔrt]
garage	гараж (ч)	[ɦa'raʒ]
private property	приватна власність (ж)	[pri'watna 'wlasnistʲ]
warning sign	попереджувальний напис (ч)	[popɛ'rɛdʒuwalʲnij 'napis]
security	охорона (ж)	[oho'rona]
security guard	охоронник (ч)	[oho'ronik]
renovations	ремонт (ч)	[rɛ'mɔnt]
to renovate (vt)	робити ремонт	[ro'biti rɛ'mɔnt]
to put in order	привести до ладу	[pri'wɛsti do 'ladu]
to paint (~ a wall)	фарбувати	[farbu'wati]
wallpaper	шпалери (мн)	[ʃpa'lɛri]

to varnish (vt)	покривати лаком	[pokri'wati 'lakom]
pipe	труба (ж)	[tru'ba]
tools	інструменти (мн)	[instru'mɛnti]
basement	підвал (ч)	[pid'wal]
sewerage (system)	каналізація (ж)	[kanali'zatsiʲa]

14. House. Apartment. Part 2

apartment	квартира (ж)	[kwar'tira]
room	кімната (ж)	[kim'nata]
bedroom	спальня (ж)	['spalʲnʲa]
dining room	їдальня (ж)	['ʲidalʲnʲa]

living room	вітальня (ж)	[wi'talʲnʲa]
study (home office)	кабінет (ч)	[kabi'nɛt]
entry room	передпокій (ч)	[pɛrɛd'pokij]
bathroom (room with a bath or shower)	ванна кімната (ж)	['wana kim'nata]

half bath	туалет (ч)	[tua'lɛt]

floor	підлога (ж)	[pid'loɦa]
ceiling	стеля (ж)	['stɛlʲa]

to dust (vt)	витирати пил	[witi'rati pil]
vacuum cleaner	пилосос (ч)	[pilo'sɔs]
to vacuum (vt)	пилососити	[pilo'sositi]

mop	швабра (ж)	['ʃwabra]
dust cloth	ганчірка (ж)	[ɦan'tʃirka]
short broom	віник (ч)	['winik]
dustpan	совок (ч) для сміття	[so'wok dlʲa smit'tʲa]

furniture	меблі (мн)	['mɛbli]
table	стіл (ч)	[stil]
chair	стілець (ч)	[sti'lɛts]
armchair	крісло (с)	['krislo]

bookcase	шафа (ж)	['ʃafa]
shelf	полиця (ж)	[po'litsʲa]
wardrobe	шафа (ж)	['ʃafa]

mirror	дзеркало (с)	['dzɛrkalo]
carpet	килим (ч)	['kilim]
fireplace	камін (ч)	[ka'min]
drapes	штори (мн)	['ʃtori]
table lamp	настільна лампа (ж)	[na'stilʲna 'lampa]
chandelier	люстра (ж)	['lʲustra]

kitchen	кухня (ж)	['kuhnʲa]
gas stove (range)	плита (ж) газова	[pli'ta 'ɦazowa]

| electric stove | плита (ж) електрична | [pli'ta ɛlɛkt'ritʃna] |
| microwave oven | мікрохвильова піч (ж) | [mikrohwiɬo'wa pitʃ] |

refrigerator	холодильник (ч)	[holo'diɬnik]
freezer	морозильник (ч)	[moro'ziɬnik]
dishwasher	посудомийна машина (ж)	[posudo'mijna ma'ʃina]
faucet	кран (ч)	[kran]

meat grinder	м'ясорубка (ж)	[mʲaso'rubka]
juicer	соковижималка (ж)	[sokowiʒi'malka]
toaster	тостер (ч)	['tɔstɛr]
mixer	міксер (ч)	['miksɛr]
coffee machine	кавоварка (ж)	[kawo'warka]
kettle	чайник (ч)	['tʃajnik]
teapot	заварник (ч)	[za'warnik]

TV set	телевізор (ч)	[tɛlɛ'wizor]
VCR (video recorder)	відеомагнітофон (ч)	['widɛo maɦnito'fɔn]
iron (e.g., steam ~)	праска (ж)	['praska]
telephone	телефон (ч)	[tɛlɛ'fɔn]

15. Professions. Social status

director	директор (ч)	[di'rɛktor]
superior	начальник (ч)	[na'tʃaɬnik]
president	президент (ч)	[prɛzi'dɛnt]
assistant	помічник (ч)	[pomitʃ'nik]
secretary	секретар (ч)	[sɛkrɛ'tar]

owner, proprietor	власник (ч)	['wlasnik]
partner	партнер (ч)	[part'nɛr]
stockholder	акціонер (ч)	[aktsio'nɛr]

businessman	бізнесмен (ч)	[biznɛs'mɛn]
millionaire	мільйонер (ч)	[miɬo'nɛr]
billionaire	мільярдер (ч)	[miljar'dɛr]

actor	актор (ч)	[ak'tor]
architect	архітектор (ч)	[arhi'tɛktor]
banker	банкір (ч)	[ba'nkir]
broker	брокер (ч)	['brɔkɛr]

veterinarian	ветеринар (ч)	[wɛtɛri'nar]
doctor	лікар (ч)	['likar]
chambermaid	покоївка (ж)	[poko'jiwka]
designer	дизайнер (ч)	[di'zajnɛr]
correspondent	кореспондент (ч)	[korɛspon'dɛnt]
delivery man	кур'єр (ч)	[ku'rʲɛr]
electrician	електрик (ч)	[ɛ'lɛktrik]

musician	музикант (ч)	[muzi'kant]
babysitter	няня (ж)	['nʲanʲa]
hairdresser	перукар (ч)	[pɛru'kar]
herder, shepherd	пастух (ч)	[pas'tuh]

singer (masc.)	співак (ч)	[spi'wak]
translator	перекладач (ч)	[pɛrɛkla'datʃ]
writer	письменник (ч)	[pisʲ'mɛnik]
carpenter	тесля (ч)	['tɛslʲa]
cook	кухар (ч)	['kuhar]

fireman	пожежник (ч)	[po'ʒɛʒnik]
police officer	поліцейський (ч)	[poli'tsɛjsʲkij]
mailman	листоноша (ч)	[listo'noʃa]
programmer	програміст (ч)	[proh'ramist]
salesman (store staff)	продавець (ч)	[proda'wɛts]

worker	робочий (ч)	[ro'botʃij]
gardener	садівник (ч)	[sadiw'nik]
plumber	сантехнік (ч)	[san'tɛhnik]
dentist	стоматолог (ч)	[stoma'toloh]
flight attendant (fem.)	стюардеса (ж)	[stʲuar'dɛsa]

dancer (masc.)	танцюрист (ч)	[tantsʲu'rist]
bodyguard	охоронець (ч)	[oho'ronɛts]
scientist	вчений (ч)	['wtʃɛnij]
schoolteacher	вчитель (ч)	['wtʃitɛlʲ]

farmer	фермер (ч)	['fɛrmɛr]
surgeon	хірург (ч)	[hi'rurh]
miner	шахтар (ч)	[ʃah'tar]
chef (kitchen chef)	шеф-кухар (ч)	[ʃɛf 'kuhar]
driver	шофер (ч)	[ʃo'fɛr]

16. Sport

kind of sports	вид спорту (ч)	[wid 'sportu]
soccer	футбол (ч)	[fut'bol]
hockey	хокей (ч)	[ho'kɛj]
basketball	баскетбол (ч)	[baskɛt'bol]
baseball	бейсбол (ч)	[bɛjs'bol]

volleyball	волейбол (ч)	[wolɛj'bol]
boxing	бокс (ч)	[boks]
wrestling	боротьба (ж)	[borotʲ'ba]
tennis	теніс (ч)	['tɛnis]
swimming	плавання (с)	['plawanʲa]

| chess | шахи (мн) | ['ʃahi] |
| running | біг (ч) | [bih] |

athletics	легка атлетика (ж)	[lɛɦ'ka at'lɛtika]
figure skating	фігурне катання (с)	[fi'ɦurnɛ ka'tanʲa]
cycling	велоспорт (ч)	[wɛlo'spɔrt]

billiards	більярд (ч)	[bi'ljard]
bodybuilding	бодібілдинг (ч)	[bodi'bildinɦ]
golf	гольф (ч)	[ɦolʲf]
scuba diving	дайвінг (ч)	['dajwinɦ]
sailing	парусний спорт (ч)	['parusnij sport]
archery	стрільба (ж) з луку	[strilʲ'ba z 'luku]

period, half	тайм (ч)	[tajm]
half-time	перерва (ж)	[pɛ'rɛrwa]
tie	нічия (ж)	[nitʃiʲa]
to tie (vi)	зіграти внічию	[zi'ɦrati wnitʃiʲu]

treadmill	бігова доріжка (ж)	[biɦo'wa do'riʒka]
player	гравець (ч)	[ɦra'wɛʦ]
substitute	запасний гравець (ч)	[zapas'nij ɦra'wɛʦ]
substitutes bench	лава (ж) запасних	['lawa zapas'niɦ]
match	матч (ч)	[matʃ]
goal	ворота (мн)	[wo'rɔta]
goalkeeper	воротар (ч)	[woro'tar]
goal (score)	гол (ч)	[ɦol]

Olympic Games	Олімпійські ігри (мн)	[olim'pijsʲki 'iɦri]
to set a record	встановлювати рекорд	[wsta'nɔwlʲuwati rɛ'kɔrd]
final	фінал (ч)	[fi'nal]
champion	чемпіон (ч)	[tʃɛmpi'ɔn]
championship	чемпіонат (ч)	[tʃɛmpio'nat]

winner	переможець (ч)	[pɛrɛ'mɔʒɛʦ]
victory	перемога (ж)	[pɛrɛ'mɔɦa]
to win (vi)	виграти	['wiɦrati]
to lose (not win)	програти	[proɦ'rati]
medal	медаль (ж)	[mɛ'dalʲ]

first place	перше місце (с)	['pɛrʃɛ 'mistsɛ]
second place	друге місце (с)	['druɦɛ 'mistsɛ]
third place	третє місце (с)	['trɛtɛ 'mistsɛ]

stadium	стадіон (ч)	[stadi'ɔn]
fan, supporter	уболівальник (ч)	[uboli'walʲnik]
trainer, coach	тренер (ч)	['trɛnɛr]
training	тренування (с)	[trɛnu'wanʲa]

17. Foreign languages. Orthography

| language | мова (ж) | ['mɔwa] |
| to study (vt) | вивчати | [wiw'tʃati] |

| pronunciation | вимова (ж) | [wɨ'mɔwa] |
| accent | акцент (ч) | [ak'ʦɛnt] |

noun	іменник (ч)	[i'mɛnɨk]
adjective	прикметник (ч)	[prɨk'mɛtnɨk]
verb	дієслово (с)	[diɛ'slɔwo]
adverb	прислівник (ч)	[prɨs'liwnɨk]

pronoun	займенник (ч)	[zaj'mɛnɨk]
interjection	вигук (ч)	['wɨɦuk]
preposition	прийменник (ч)	[prɨj'mɛnɨk]

root	корінь (ч) слова	['kɔrinʲ 'slɔwa]
ending	закінчення (с)	[za'kintʃɛnʲa]
prefix	префікс (ч)	['prɛfiks]
syllable	склад (ч)	['sklad]
suffix	суфікс (ч)	['sufiks]

stress mark	наголос (ч)	['naɦolos]
period, dot	крапка (ж)	['krapka]
comma	кома (ж)	['kɔma]
colon	двокрапка (ж)	[dwo'krapka]
ellipsis	крапки (мн)	[krap'kɨ]

question	питання (с)	[pɨ'tanʲa]
question mark	знак (ч) питання	[znak pɨ'tanʲa]
exclamation point	знак (ч) оклику	[znak 'ɔklɨku]

in quotation marks	в лапках	[w lap'kah]
in parenthesis	в дужках	[w duʒ'kah]
letter	літера (ж)	['litɛra]
capital letter	велика літера (ж)	[wɛ'lɨka 'litɛra]

sentence	речення (с)	['rɛtʃɛnʲa]
group of words	словосполучення (с)	[slowospo'lutʃɛnʲa]
expression	вислів (ч)	['wɨsliw]

subject	підмет (ч)	['pidmɛt]
predicate	присудок (ч)	['prɨsudok]
line	рядок (ч)	[rʲa'dɔk]
paragraph	абзац (ч)	[ab'zaʦ]

synonym	синонім (ч)	[sɨ'nɔnim]
antonym	антонім (ч)	[an'tɔnim]
exception	виняток (ч)	['wɨnʲatok]
to underline (vt)	підкреслити	[pid'krɛslɨtɨ]

rules	правила (мн)	['prawɨla]
grammar	граматика (ж)	[ɦra'matɨka]
vocabulary	лексика (ж)	['lɛksɨka]
phonetics	фонетика (ж)	[fo'nɛtɨka]
alphabet	алфавіт (ч)	[alfa'wit]

textbook	підручник (ч)	[pid'rutʃnik]
dictionary	словник (ч)	[slow'nik]
phrasebook	розмовник (ч)	[roz'mɔwnik]

word	слово (с)	['slɔwo]
meaning	сенс (ч)	[sɛns]
memory	пам'ять (ж)	['pamʲʲatʲ]

18. The Earth. Geography

the Earth	Земля (ж)	[zɛm'lʲa]
the globe (the Earth)	земна куля (ж)	[zɛm'na 'kulʲa]
planet	планета (ж)	[pla'nɛta]

geography	географія (ж)	[ɦɛo'ɦrafiʲa]
nature	природа (ж)	[pri'rɔda]
map	карта (ж)	['karta]
atlas	атлас (ч)	['atlas]

in the north	на півночі	[na 'piwnotʃi]
in the south	на півдні	[na 'piwdni]
in the west	на заході	[na 'zahodi]
in the east	на сході	[na 'shɔdi]

sea	море (с)	['mɔrɛ]
ocean	океан (ч)	[okɛ'an]
gulf (bay)	затока (ж)	[za'tɔka]
straits	протока (ж)	[pro'tɔka]

continent (mainland)	материк (ч)	[matɛ'rik]
island	острів (ч)	['ɔstriw]
peninsula	півострів (ч)	[pi'wɔstriw]
archipelago	архіпелаг (ч)	[arhipɛ'laɦ]

harbor	гавань (ж)	['ɦawanʲ]
coral reef	кораловий риф (ч)	[ko'ralowij rif]
shore	берег (ч)	['bɛrɛɦ]
coast	узбережжя (с)	[uzbɛ'rɛʑa]

| flow (flood tide) | приплив (ч) | [prip'liw] |
| ebb (ebb tide) | відплив (ч) | [wid'pliw] |

latitude	широта (ж)	[ʃiro'ta]
longitude	довгота (ж)	[dowɦo'ta]
parallel	паралель (ж)	[para'lɛlʲ]
equator	екватор (ч)	[ɛk'wator]

sky	небо (с)	['nɛbo]
horizon	горизонт (ч)	[ɦori'zɔnt]
atmosphere	атмосфера (ж)	[atmos'fɛra]

mountain	гора (ж)	[ɦoˈra]
summit, top	вершина (ж)	[wɛrˈʃina]
cliff	скеля (ж)	[ˈskɛlʲa]
hill	горб (ч)	[ɦorb]

volcano	вулкан (ч)	[wulˈkan]
glacier	льодовик (ч)	[lʲodoˈwik]
waterfall	водоспад (ч)	[wodosˈpad]
plain	рівнина (ж)	[riwˈnina]

river	ріка (ж)	[ˈrika]
spring (natural source)	джерело (с)	[dʒɛrɛˈlɔ]
bank (of river)	берег (ч)	[ˈbɛrɛɦ]
downstream (adv)	вниз за течією (ж)	[wniz za ˈtɛtʃiɛʲu]
upstream (adv)	уверх по течії	[uˈwɛrh po ˈtɛtʃiji]

lake	озеро (с)	[ˈɔzɛro]
dam	гребля (ж)	[ˈɦrɛblʲa]
canal	канал (ч)	[kaˈnal]
swamp (marshland)	болото (с)	[boˈlɔto]
ice	крига (ж)	[ˈkriɦa]

19. Countries of the world. Part 1

Europe	Європа (ж)	[ɛwˈrɔpa]
European Union	Європейський Союз (ч)	[ɛwroˈpɛjsʲkij soˈʲuz]
European (n)	європеєць (ч)	[ɛwroˈpɛɛʦ]
European (adj)	європейський	[ɛwroˈpɛjsʲkij]

Austria	Австрія (ж)	[ˈawstriʲa]
Great Britain	Великобританія (ж)	[wɛlikobriˈtaniʲa]
England	Англія (ж)	[ˈanɦliʲa]
Belgium	Бельгія (ж)	[ˈbɛlʲɦiʲa]
Germany	Німеччина (ж)	[niˈmɛtʃina]

Netherlands	Нідерланди (ж)	[nidɛrˈlandi]
Holland	Голландія (ж)	[ɦoˈlandiʲa]
Greece	Греція (ж)	[ˈɦrɛtsiʲa]
Denmark	Данія (ж)	[ˈdaniʲa]
Ireland	Ірландія (ж)	[irˈlandiʲa]

Iceland	Ісландія (ж)	[isˈlandiʲa]
Spain	Іспанія (ж)	[ispaniʲa]
Italy	Італія (ж)	[iˈtaliʲa]
Cyprus	Кіпр (ж)	[kipr]
Malta	Мальта (ж)	[ˈmalʲta]

Norway	Норвегія (ж)	[norˈwɛɦiʲa]
Portugal	Португалія (ж)	[portuˈɦaliʲa]
Finland	Фінляндія (ж)	[finˈlʲandiʲa]

| France | Франція (ж) | ['frantsiⁱa] |
| Sweden | Швеція (ж) | ['ʃwɛtsiⁱa] |

Switzerland	Швейцарія (ж)	[ʃwɛj'tsariⁱa]
Scotland	Шотландія (ж)	[ʃot'landiⁱa]
Vatican	Ватикан (ч)	[wati'kan]
Liechtenstein	Ліхтенштейн (ч)	[lihtɛn'ʃtɛjn]
Luxembourg	Люксембург (ч)	[lʲuksɛm'burɦ]

Monaco	Монако (с)	[mo'nako]
Albania	Албанія (ж)	[al'baniⁱa]
Bulgaria	Болгарія (ж)	[bol'ɦariⁱa]
Hungary	Угорщина (ж)	[u'ɦorɕina]
Latvia	Латвія (ж)	['latwiⁱa]

Lithuania	Литва (ж)	[lɨt'wa]
Poland	Польща (ж)	['polʲɕa]
Romania	Румунія (ж)	[ru'muniⁱa]
Serbia	Сербія (ж)	['sɛrbiⁱa]
Slovakia	Словаччина (ж)	[slo'watʃina]

Croatia	Хорватія (ж)	[hor'watiⁱa]
Czech Republic	Чехія (ж)	['tʃɛhiⁱa]
Estonia	Естонія (ж)	[ɛs'toniⁱa]
Bosnia and Herzegovina	Боснія (ж)	['bɔsniⁱa]
	і Герцеговина (ж)	і ɦɛrtsɛɦo'wɨna]
Macedonia (Republic of ~)	Македонія (ж)	[makɛ'dɔniⁱa]

Slovenia	Словенія (ж)	[slo'wɛniⁱa]
Montenegro	Чорногорія (ж)	[tʃorno'ɦoriⁱa]
Belarus	Білорусь (ж)	[bilo'rusʲ]
Moldova, Moldavia	Молдова (ж)	[mol'dɔwa]
Russia	Росія (ж)	[ro'siⁱa]
Ukraine	Україна (ж)	[ukra'jɨna]

20. Countries of the world. Part 2

Asia	Азія (ж)	['aziⁱa]
Vietnam	В'єтнам (ч)	[wʲɛt'nam]
India	Індія (ж)	['indiⁱa]
Israel	Ізраїль (ч)	[iz'rajilʲ]
China	Китай (ч)	[kiⁱ'taj]

Lebanon	Ліван (ч)	[li'wan]
Mongolia	Монголія (ж)	[mon'ɦoliⁱa]
Malaysia	Малайзія (ж)	[ma'lajziⁱa]
Pakistan	Пакистан (ч)	[paki'stan]
Saudi Arabia	Саудівська Аравія (ж)	[sa'udiwsʲka a'rawiⁱa]
Thailand	Таїланд (ч)	[taji'land]
Taiwan	Тайвань (ч)	[taj'wanʲ]

Turkey	Туреччина (ж)	[tu'rɛtʃina]
Japan	Японія (ж)	[ja'poniˌa]
Afghanistan	Афганістан (ч)	[afhani'stan]

Bangladesh	Бангладеш (ч)	[banhla'dɛʃ]
Indonesia	Індонезія (ж)	[indo'nɛziˌa]
Jordan	Йорданія (ж)	[ˌor'daniˌa]
Iraq	Ірак (ч)	[i'rak]
Iran	Іран (ч)	[i'ran]

Cambodia	Камбоджа (ж)	[kam'bɔdʒa]
Kuwait	Кувейт (ч)	[ku'wɛjt]
Laos	Лаос (ч)	[la'ɔs]
Myanmar	М'янма (ж)	['mˀˌanma]
Nepal	Непал (ч)	[nɛ'pal]

United Arab Emirates	Об'єднані Арабські емірати	[o'bˀɛdnani a'rabsˌki ɛmi'rati]
Syria	Сирія (ж)	['siriˌa]
Palestine	Палестинська автономія (ж)	[palɛ'stinsˌka awto'nomiˌa]
South Korea	Південна Корея (ж)	[piw'dɛna ko'rɛˌa]
North Korea	Північна Корея (ж)	[piw'nitʃna ko'rɛˌa]

United States of America	Сполучені Штати Америки	[spo'lutʃɛni 'ʃtatɨ a'mɛriki]
Canada	Канада (ж)	[ka'nada]
Mexico	Мексика (ж)	['mɛksɨka]

| Argentina | Аргентина (ж) | [arhɛn'tina] |
| Brazil | Бразилія (ж) | [bra'zɨliˌa] |

Colombia	Колумбія (ж)	[ko'lumbiˌa]
Cuba	Куба (ж)	['kuba]
Chile	Чилі (ж)	['tʃɨli]

| Venezuela | Венесуела (ж) | [wɛnɛsu'ɛla] |
| Ecuador | Еквадор (ч) | [ɛkwa'dɔr] |

The Bahamas	Багамські острови (мн)	[ba'hamsˌki ostro'wɨ]
Panama	Панама (ж)	[pa'nama]
Egypt	Єгипет (ч)	[ɛ'hiˌpɛt]

| Morocco | Марокко (с) | [ma'rɔkko] |
| Tunisia | Туніс (ч) | [tu'nis] |

Kenya	Кенія (ж)	['kɛniˌa]
Libya	Лівія (ж)	['liwiˌa]
South Africa	Південно-Африканська Республіка (ж)	[piw'dɛno afri'kansˌka rɛs'publika]
Australia	Австралія (ж)	[aw'straliˌa]
New Zealand	Нова Зеландія (ж)	[no'wa zɛ'landiˌa]

21. Weather. Natural disasters

weather	погода (ж)	[po'ɦoda]
weather forecast	прогноз (ч) погоди (ж)	[proɦ'nɔz po'ɦodɨ]
temperature	температура (ж)	[tɛmpɛra'tura]
thermometer	термометр (ч)	[tɛr'mɔmɛtr]
barometer	барометр (ч)	[ba'rɔmɛtr]
sun	сонце (с)	['sɔnʦɛ]
to shine (vi)	світити	[swi'tɨti]
sunny (day)	сонячний	['sɔnʲaʧnɨj]
to come up (vi)	зійти	[zij'tɨ]
to set (vi)	сісти	['sistɨ]
rain	дощ (ч)	[dɔç]
it's raining	йде дощ	[jdɛ dɔç]
pouring rain	проливний дощ (ч)	[prolɨw'nɨj dɔç]
rain cloud	хмара (ж)	['hmara]
puddle	калюжа (ж)	[ka'lʲuʒa]
to get wet (in rain)	мокнути	['mɔknutɨ]
thunderstorm	гроза (ж)	[ɦro'za]
lightning (~ strike)	блискавка (ж)	['blɨskawka]
to flash (vi)	блискати	['blɨskatɨ]
thunder	грім (ч)	[ɦrim]
it's thundering	гримить грім	[ɦrɨ'mɨtʲ ɦrim]
hail	град (ч)	[ɦrad]
it's hailing	йде град	[jdɛ ɦrad]
heat (extreme ~)	спека (ж)	['spɛka]
it's hot	спекотно	[spɛ'kɔtno]
it's warm	тепло	['tɛplo]
it's cold	холодно	['hɔlodno]
fog (mist)	туман (ч)	[tu'man]
foggy	туманний	[tu'manɨj]
cloud	хмара (ж)	['hmara]
cloudy (adj)	хмарний	['hmarnɨj]
humidity	вологість (ж)	[wolo'ɦistʲ]
snow	сніг (ч)	[sniɦ]
it's snowing	йде сніг (ч)	[jdɛ sniɦ]
frost (severe ~, freezing cold)	мороз (ч)	[mo'rɔz]
below zero (adv)	нижче нуля	['nɨʒʧɛ nu'lʲa]
hoarfrost	паморозь (ж)	['pamorozʲ]
bad weather	негода (ж)	[nɛ'ɦoda]
disaster	катастрофа (ж)	[kata'strɔfa]
flood, inundation	повінь (ж)	['pɔwinʲ]
avalanche	лавина (ж)	[la'wɨna]

earthquake	землетрус (ч)	[zɛmlɛt'rus]
tremor, quake	поштовх (ч)	['pɔʃtowh]
epicenter	епіцентр (ч)	[ɛpi'tsɛntr]
eruption	виверження (с)	['wiwɛrʒɛnʲa]
lava	лава (ж)	['lawa]

tornado	торнадо (ч)	[tor'nado]
twister	смерч (ч)	[smɛrtʃ]
hurricane	ураган (ч)	[urahan]
tsunami	цунамі (с)	[tsu'nami]
cyclone	циклон (ч)	[tsɨk'lɔn]

22. Animals. Part 1

| animal | тварина (ж) | [twa'rina] |
| predator | хижак (ч) | [hɨ'ʒak] |

tiger	тигр (ч)	[tɨɦr]
lion	лев (ч)	[lɛw]
wolf	вовк (ч)	[wowk]
fox	лисиця (ж)	[lɨ'sɨtsʲa]
jaguar	ягуар (ч)	[jaɦu'ar]

lynx	рись (ж)	[risʲ]
coyote	койот (ч)	[ko'jot]
jackal	шакал (ч)	[ʃa'kal]
hyena	гієна (ж)	[ɦi'ɛna]

squirrel	білка (ж)	['bilka]
hedgehog	їжак (ч)	[jɨ'ʒak]
rabbit	кріль (ч)	[krilʲ]
raccoon	єнот (ч)	[ɛ'nɔt]

hamster	хом'як (ч)	[ho'mʔʲak]
mole	кріт (ч)	[krit]
mouse	миша (ж)	['miʃa]
rat	щур (ч)	[ɕur]
bat	кажан (ч)	[ka'ʒan]

beaver	бобер (ч)	[bo'bɛr]
horse	кінь (ч)	[kinʲ]
deer	олень (ч)	['ɔlɛnʲ]
camel	верблюд (ч)	[wɛr'blʲud]
zebra	зебра (ж)	['zɛbra]

whale	кит (ч)	[kit]
seal	тюлень (ч)	[tʲu'lɛnʲ]
walrus	морж (ч)	[morʒ]
dolphin	дельфін (ч)	[dɛlʲ'fin]
bear	ведмідь (ч)	[wɛd'midʲ]

monkey	мавпа (ж)	['mawpa]
elephant	слон (ч)	[slon]
rhinoceros	носоріг (ч)	[noso'riɦ]
giraffe	жирафа (ж)	[ʒɨrafa]

hippopotamus	бегемот (ч)	[bɛɦɛ'mɔt]
kangaroo	кенгуру (ч)	[kɛnɦu'ru]
cat	кішка (ж)	['kiʃka]

cow	корова (ж)	[ko'rɔwa]
bull	бик (ч)	[bɨk]
sheep (ewe)	вівця (ж)	[wiw'tsʲa]
goat	коза (ж)	[ko'za]

donkey	осел (ч)	[o'sɛl]
pig, hog	свиня (ж)	[swɨ'nʲa]
hen (chicken)	курка (ж)	['kurka]
rooster	півень (ч)	['piwɛnʲ]

duck	качка (ж)	['katʃka]
goose	гусак (ч)	[ɦu'sak]
turkey (hen)	індичка (ж)	[in'diʧka]
sheepdog	вівчарка (ж)	[wiw'tʃarka]

23. Animals. Part 2

bird	птах (ч)	[ptaɦ]
pigeon	голуб (ч)	['ɦolub]
sparrow	горобець (ч)	[ɦoro'bɛʦ]
tit (great tit)	синиця (ж)	[sɨ'nɨʦʲa]
magpie	сорока (ж)	[so'rɔka]

eagle	орел (ч)	[o'rɛl]
hawk	яструб (ч)	['ʲastrub]
falcon	сокіл (ч)	['sɔkil]

swan	лебідь (ч)	['lɛbidʲ]
crane	журавель (ч)	[ʒura'wɛlʲ]
stork	чорногуз (ч)	[ʧorno'ɦuz]
parrot	папуга (ч)	[pa'puɦa]
peacock	пава (ж)	['pawa]
ostrich	страус (ч)	['straus]

heron	чапля (ж)	['ʧaplʲa]
nightingale	соловей (ч)	[solo'wɛj]
swallow	ластівка (ж)	['lastiwka]
woodpecker	дятел (ч)	['dʲatɛl]
cuckoo	зозуля (ж)	[zo'zulʲa]
owl	сова (ж)	[so'wa]
penguin	пінгвін (ч)	[pinɦ'win]

tuna	тунець (ч)	[tu'nɛts]
trout	форель (ж)	[fo'rɛlʲ]
eel	вугор (ч)	[wu'ɦɔr]

shark	акула (ж)	[a'kula]
crab	краб (ч)	[krab]
jellyfish	медуза (ж)	[mɛ'duza]
octopus	восьминіг (ч)	[wosʲmi'niɦ]

starfish	морська зірка (ж)	[morsʲˈka 'zirka]
sea urchin	морський їжак (ч)	[morsʲˈkij jiˈʒak]
seahorse	морський коник (ч)	[morsʲˈkij 'konik]
shrimp	креветка (ж)	[krɛ'wɛtka]

snake	змія (ж)	[zmiˈʲa]
viper	гадюка (ж)	[ɦa'dʲuka]
lizard	ящірка (ж)	[ˈʲaɕirka]
iguana	ігуана (ж)	[iɦu'ana]
chameleon	хамелеон (ч)	[ɦamɛlɛ'ɔn]
scorpion	скорпіон (ч)	[skorpi'ɔn]

turtle	черепаха (ж)	[ʧɛrɛ'paɦa]
frog	жабка (ж)	[ˈʒabka]
crocodile	крокодил (ч)	[kroko'dɨl]

insect, bug	комаха (ж)	[ko'maɦa]
butterfly	метелик (ч)	[mɛ'tɛlik]
ant	мураха (ж)	[mu'raɦa]
fly	муха (ж)	[ˈmuɦa]

mosquito	комар (ч)	[ko'mar]
beetle	жук (ч)	[ʒuk]
bee	бджола (ж)	[bdʒo'la]
spider	павук (ч)	[pa'wuk]

24. Trees. Plants

tree	дерево (с)	[ˈdɛrɛwo]
birch	береза (ж)	[bɛ'rɛza]
oak	дуб (ч)	[dub]
linden tree	липа (ж)	[ˈlɨpa]
aspen	осика (ж)	[o'sɨka]

maple	клен (ч)	[klɛn]
spruce	ялина (ж)	[ja'lɨna]
pine	сосна (ж)	[sos'na]
cedar	кедр (ч)	[kɛdr]

| poplar | тополя (ж) | [to'pɔlʲa] |
| rowan | горобина (ж) | [ɦoro'bɨna] |

beech	бук (ч)	[buk]
elm	в'яз (ч)	[wʲˈaz]
ash (tree)	ясен (ч)	[ˈʲasɛn]
chestnut	каштан (ч)	[kaʃˈtan]
palm tree	пальма (ж)	[ˈpalʲma]
bush	кущ (ч)	[kuɕ]
mushroom	гриб (ч)	[ɦrib]
poisonous mushroom	отруйний гриб (ч)	[otˈrujnij ɦrib]
cep (Boletus edulis)	білий гриб (ч)	[ˈbilij ˈɦrib]
russula	сироїжка (ж)	[siroˈjiʒka]
fly agaric	мухомор (ч)	[muhoˈmɔr]
death cap	поганка (ж)	[poˈɦanka]
flower	квітка (ж)	[ˈkwitka]
bouquet (of flowers)	букет (ч)	[buˈkɛt]
rose (flower)	троянда (ж)	[troˈʲanda]
tulip	тюльпан (ч)	[tʲulʲˈpan]
carnation	гвоздика (ж)	[ɦwozˈdika]
camomile	ромашка (ж)	[roˈmaʃka]
cactus	кактус (ч)	[ˈkaktus]
lily of the valley	конвалія (ж)	[konˈwaliʲa]
snowdrop	пролісок (ч)	[ˈprɔlisok]
water lily	латаття (с)	[laˈtattʲa]
greenhouse (tropical ~)	оранжерея (ж)	[oranʒɛˈrɛʲa]
lawn	газон (ч)	[ɦaˈzɔn]
flowerbed	клумба (ж)	[ˈklumba]
plant	рослина (ж)	[rosˈlina]
grass	трава (ж)	[traˈwa]
leaf	листок (ч)	[lisˈtɔk]
petal	пелюстка (ж)	[pɛˈlʲustka]
stem	стебло (с)	[stɛbˈlo]
young plant (shoot)	паросток (ч)	[ˈparostok]
cereal crops	зернові рослини (мн)	[zɛrnoˈwi rosˈlini]
wheat	пшениця (ж)	[pʃɛˈnitsʲa]
rye	жито (с)	[ˈʒito]
oats	овес (ч)	[oˈwɛs]
millet	просо (с)	[ˈprɔso]
barley	ячмінь (ч)	[jatʲˈminʲ]
corn	кукурудза (ж)	[kukuˈrudza]
rice	рис (ч)	[ris]

25. Various useful words

balance (of situation)	баланс (ч)	[baˈlans]
base (basis)	база (ж)	[ˈbaza]

beginning	початок (ч)	[po'tʃatok]
category	категорія (ж)	[katɛ'ɦoriˈa]
choice	вибір (ч)	['wibir]
coincidence	збіг (ч)	[zbiɦ]
comparison	порівняння (с)	[poriw'nˈanˈa]
degree (extent, amount)	ступінь (ч)	['stupinˈ]
development	розвиток (ч)	['rɔzwitok]
difference	різниця (ж)	[riz'nitsˈa]
effect (e.g., of drugs)	ефект (ч)	[ɛ'fɛkt]
effort (exertion)	зусилля (с)	[zu'siłˈa]
element	елемент (ч)	[ɛlɛ'mɛnt]
example (illustration)	приклад (ч)	['priklad]
fact	факт (ч)	[fakt]
help	допомога (ж)	[dopo'mɔɦa]
ideal	ідеал (ч)	[idɛ'al]
kind (sort, type)	вид (ч)	[wid]
mistake, error	помилка (ж)	[po'miłka]
moment	момент (ч)	[mo'mɛnt]
obstacle	перешкода (ж)	[pɛrɛʃ'kɔda]
part (~ of sth)	частина (ж)	[tʃas'tina]
pause (break)	пауза (ж)	['pauza]
position	позиція (ж)	[po'zitsiˈa]
problem	проблема (ж)	[prob'lɛma]
process	процес (ч)	[pro'tsɛs]
progress	прогрес (ч)	[proɦ'rɛs]
property (quality)	властивість (ж)	[wlas'tiwistˈ]
reaction	реакція (ж)	[rɛ'aktsiˈa]
risk	ризик (ч)	['rizik]
secret	таємниця (ж)	[taɛm'nitsˈa]
series	серія (ж)	['sɛriˈa]
shape (outer form)	форма (ж)	['fɔrma]
situation	ситуація (ж)	[situ'atsiˈa]
solution	рішення (с)	['riʃɛnˈa]
standard (adj)	стандартний	[stan'dartnij]
stop (pause)	перерва (ж)	[pɛ'rɛrwa]
style	стиль (ч)	[stiłˈ]
system	система (ж)	[sis'tɛma]
table (chart)	таблиця (ж)	[tab'litsˈa]
tempo, rate	темп (ч)	[tɛmp]
term (word, expression)	термін (ч)	['tɛrmin]
truth (e.g., moment of ~)	істина (ж)	['istina]

| turn (please wait your ~) | черга (ж) | [ˈtʃɛrɦa] |
| urgent (adj) | терміновий | [tɛrmiˈnɔwɨj] |

utility (usefulness)	користь (ж)	[ˈkɔrɨstʲ]
variant (alternative)	варіант (ч)	[wariˈant]
way (means, method)	спосіб (ч)	[ˈspɔsib]
zone	зона (ж)	[ˈzɔna]

26. Modifiers. Adjectives. Part 1

additional (adj)	додатковий	[dodatˈkɔwɨj]
ancient (~ civilization)	давній	[ˈdawnij]
artificial (adj)	штучний	[ˈʃtutʃnɨj]
bad (adj)	поганий	[poˈɦanɨj]
beautiful (person)	гарний	[ˈɦarnɨj]

big (in size)	великий	[wɛˈlɨkɨj]
bitter (taste)	гіркий	[ɦirˈkɨj]
blind (sightless)	сліпий	[sliˈpɨj]
central (adj)	центральний	[tsɛnˈtralʲnɨj]

children's (adj)	дитячий	[dɨˈtʲatʃɨj]
clandestine (secret)	підпільний	[pidˈpilʲnɨj]
clean (free from dirt)	чистий	[ˈtʃistɨj]
clever (smart)	розумний	[roˈzumnɨj]
compatible (adj)	сумісний	[suˈmisnɨj]

contented (satisfied)	задоволений	[zadoˈwɔlɛnɨj]
dangerous (adj)	небезпечний	[nɛbɛzˈpɛtʃnɨj]
dead (not alive)	мертвий	[ˈmɛrtwɨj]
dense (fog, smoke)	щільний	[ˈɕilʲnɨj]
difficult (decision)	важкий	[waʒˈkɨj]

dirty (not clean)	брудний	[brudˈnɨj]
easy (not difficult)	легкий	[lɛɦˈkɨj]
empty (glass, room)	пустий	[pusˈtɨj]
exact (amount)	точний	[ˈtɔtʃnɨj]
excellent (adj)	добрий	[ˈdɔbrɨj]

excessive (adj)	надмірний	[nadˈmirnɨj]
exterior (adj)	зовнішній	[ˈzɔwniʃnij]
fast (quick)	швидкий	[ʃwɨdˈkɨj]
fertile (land, soil)	родючий	[roˈdʲutʃij]
fragile (china, glass)	крихкий	[krɨhˈkɨj]

free (at no cost)	безкоштовний	[bɛzkoʃˈtɔwnɨj]
fresh (~ water)	прісний	[ˈprisnɨj]
frozen (food)	заморожений	[zamoˈrɔʒɛnɨj]
full (completely filled)	повний	[ˈpɔwnɨj]
happy (adj)	щасливий	[ɕasˈlɨwɨj]

hard (not soft)	твердий	[twɛr'dij]
huge (adj)	величезний	[wɛli'tʃɛznij]
ill (sick, unwell)	хворий	['hwɔrij]
immobile (adj)	нерухомий	[nɛru'hɔmij]
important (adj)	важливий	[waʒ'liwij]

interior (adj)	внутрішній	['wnutriʃnij]
last (e.g., ~ week)	минулий	[mi'nulij]
last (final)	останній	[os'tanij]
left (e.g., ~ side)	лівий	['liwij]
legal (legitimate)	законний	[za'kɔnij]

light (in weight)	легкий	[lɛɦ'kij]
liquid (fluid)	рідкий	[rid'kij]
long (e.g., ~ hair)	довгий	['dɔwɦij]
loud (voice, etc.)	гучний	[ɦutʃ'nij]
low (voice)	тихий	['tiɦij]

27. Modifiers. Adjectives. Part 2

main (principal)	головний	[ɦolow'nij]
matt, matte	матовий	['matowij]
mysterious (adj)	загадковий	[zaɦad'kɔwij]
narrow (street, etc.)	вузький	[wuz'ʲkij]
native (~ country)	рідний	['ridnij]

negative (~ response)	негативний	[nɛɦa'tiwnij]
new (adj)	новий	[no'wij]
next (e.g., ~ week)	наступний	[na'stupnij]
normal (adj)	нормальний	[nor'malʲnij]
not difficult (adj)	неважкий	[nɛwaʒ'kij]

obligatory (adj)	обов'язковий	[obowʲʲaz'kɔwij]
old (house)	старий	[sta'rij]
open (adj)	відкритий	[wid'kritij]
opposite (adj)	протилежний	[proti'lɛʒnij]
ordinary (usual)	звичайний	[zwi'tʃajnij]

original (unusual)	оригінальний	[oriɦi'nalʲnij]
personal (adj)	персональний	[pɛrso'nalʲnij]
polite (adj)	ввічливий	['wvitʃliwij]
poor (not rich)	бідний	['bidnij]

possible (adj)	можливий	[moʒ'liwij]
principal (main)	основний	[osnow'nij]
probable (adj)	імовірний	[imo'wirnij]
prolonged (e.g., ~ applause)	тривалий	[tri'walij]
public (open to all)	громадський	[ɦro'madsʲkij]
rare (adj)	рідкісний	['ridkisnij]

raw (uncooked)	сирий	[si'rij]
right (not left)	правий	['prawɨj]
ripe (fruit)	дозрілий	[do'zrilɨj]

risky (adj)	ризикований	[rɨzi'kowanɨj]
sad (~ look)	сумний	[sum'nɨj]
second hand (adj)	уживаний	[u'ʒiwanɨj]
shallow (water)	мілкий	[mil'kij]
sharp (blade, etc.)	гострий	['ɦostrɨj]

short (in length)	короткий	[ko'rotkij]
similar (adj)	схожий	['shoʒij]
smooth (surface)	гладкий	['ɦladkij]
soft (~ toys)	м'який	[mʲa'kij]

solid (~ wall)	міцний	[mits'nɨj]
sour (flavor, taste)	кислий	['kislɨj]
spacious (house, etc.)	просторий	[pros'torij]
special (adj)	спеціальний	[spɛtsi'alʲnɨj]

straight (line, road)	прямий	[prʲa'mɨj]
strong (person)	сильний	['silʲnɨj]
stupid (foolish)	дурний	[dur'nɨj]
superb, perfect (adj)	чудовий	[ʧu'dowɨj]

sweet (sugary)	солодкий	[so'lodkij]
tan (adj)	засмаглий	[zas'maɦlɨj]
tasty (delicious)	смачний	[smaʧ'nɨj]
unclear (adj)	неясний	[nɛ'ʲasnɨj]

28. Verbs. Part 1

to accuse (vt)	звинувачувати	[zwɨnu'waʧuwati]
to agree (say yes)	погоджуватися	[po'ɦoʤuwatisʲa]
to announce (vt)	оголошувати	[oɦo'loʃuwati]
to answer (vi, vt)	відповідати	[widpowi'dati]
to apologize (vi)	вибачатися	[wiba'ʧatisʲa]

to arrive (vi)	приїжджати	[prɨji'ʒati]
to ask (~ oneself)	запитувати	[za'pɨtuwati]
to be absent	бути відсутнім	['butɨ wid'sutnim]
to be afraid	боятися	[bo'ʲatisʲa]
to be born	народитися	[naro'ditisʲa]

to be in a hurry	поспішати	[pospi'ʃati]
to beat (to hit)	бити	['bɨti]
to begin (vt)	починати	[poʧi'nati]
to believe (in God)	вірити	['wiriti]
to belong to ...	належати	[na'lɛʒati]
to break (split into pieces)	ламати	[la'mati]

to build (vt)	будувати	[budu'wati]
to buy (purchase)	купляти	[kup'lʲati]
can (v aux)	могти	[moɦ'ti]
can (v aux)	могти	[moɦ'ti]
to cancel (call off)	скасувати	[skasu'wati]

to catch (vt)	ловити	[lo'witi]
to change (vt)	поміняти	[pomi'nʲati]
to check (to examine)	перевіряти	[pɛrɛwi'rʲati]
to choose (select)	вибирати	[wibi'rati]
to clean up (tidy)	прибирати	[pribi'rati]

to close (vt)	закривати	[zakri'wati]
to compare (vt)	зрівнювати	['zriwnʲuwati]
to complain (vi, vt)	скаржитися	['skarʒitisʲa]
to confirm (vt)	підтвердити	[pid'twɛrditi]
to congratulate (vt)	вітати	[wi'tati]

to cook (dinner)	готувати	[ɦotu'wati]
to copy (vt)	скопіювати	[skopiʲu'wati]
to cost (vt)	коштувати	['kɔʃtuwati]
to count (add up)	лічити	[li'tʃiti]
to count on ...	розраховувати на ...	[rozra'ɦowuwati na]

to create (vt)	створити	[stwo'riti]
to cry (weep)	плакати	['plakati]
to dance (vi, vt)	танцювати	[tantsʲu'wati]
to deceive (vi, vt)	обманювати	[ob'manʲuwati]
to decide (~ to do sth)	вирішувати	[wi'riʃuwati]

to delete (vt)	видалити	['widaliti]
to demand (request firmly)	вимагати	[wima'ɦati]
to deny (vt)	заперечувати	[zapɛ'rɛtʃuwati]
to depend on ...	залежати	[za'lɛʒati]
to despise (vt)	зневажати	[znɛwa'ʒati]

to die (vi)	померти	[po'mɛrti]
to dig (vt)	рити	['riti]
to disappear (vi)	зникнути	['zniknuti]
to discuss (vt)	обговорювати	[obɦo'worʲuwati]
to disturb (vt)	заважати	[zawa'ʒati]

29. Verbs. Part 2

to dive (vi)	пірнати	[pir'nati]
to divorce (vi)	розлучитися	[rozlu'tʃitisʲa]
to do (vt)	робити	[ro'biti]
to doubt (have doubts)	сумніватися	[sumni'watisʲa]
to drink (vi, vt)	пити	['piti]
to drop (let fall)	упускати	[upus'kati]

to dry (clothes, hair)	сушити	[suˈʃiti]
to eat (vi, vt)	їсти	[ˈjisti]
to end (~ a relationship)	припиняти	[pripiˈnʲati]
to excuse (forgive)	вибачати	[wibaˈtʃati]
to exist (vi)	існувати	[isnuˈwati]
to expect (foresee)	передбачити	[pɛrɛdˈbatʃiti]
to explain (vt)	пояснювати	[poˈʲasnʲuwati]
to fall (vi)	падати	[ˈpadati]
to fight (street fight, etc.)	битися	[ˈbitisʲa]
to find (vt)	знаходити	[znaˈhɔditi]
to finish (vt)	закінчувати	[zaˈkintʃuwati]
to fly (vi)	летіти	[lɛˈtiti]
to forbid (vt)	заборонити	[zaboroˈniti]
to forget (vi, vt)	забувати	[zabuˈwati]
to forgive (vt)	прощати	[proˈɕati]
to get tired	втомлюватися	[ˈwtɔmlʲuwatisʲa]
to give (vt)	давати	[daˈwati]
to go (on foot)	йти	[jti]
to hate (vt)	ненавидіти	[nɛnaˈwiditi]
to have (vt)	мати	[ˈmati]
to have breakfast	снідати	[ˈsnidati]
to have dinner	вечеряти	[wɛˈtʃɛrʲati]
to have lunch	обідати	[oˈbidati]
to hear (vt)	чути	[ˈtʃuti]
to help (vt)	допомагати	[dopomaˈhati]
to hide (vt)	ховати	[hoˈwati]
to hope (vi, vt)	сподіватися	[spodiˈwatisʲa]
to hunt (vi, vt)	полювати	[polʲuˈwati]
to hurry (vi)	поспішати	[pospiˈʃati]
to insist (vi, vt)	наполягати	[napolʲaˈhati]
to insult (vt)	ображати	[obraˈʒati]
to invite (vt)	запрошувати	[zaˈproʃuwati]
to joke (vi)	жартувати	[ʒartuˈwati]
to keep (vt)	зберігати	[zbɛriˈhati]
to kill (vt)	убивати	[ubiˈwati]
to know (sb)	знати	[ˈznati]
to know (sth)	знати	[ˈznati]
to like (I like …)	подобатися	[poˈdobatisʲa]
to look at …	дивитися	[diˈwitisʲa]
to lose (umbrella, etc.)	губити	[huˈbiti]
to love (sb)	кохати	[koˈhati]
to make a mistake	помилятися	[pomiˈlʲatisʲa]
to meet (vi, vt)	зустрічатися	[zustriˈtʃatisʲa]
to miss (school, etc.)	пропускати	[propusˈkati]

30. Verbs. Part 3

to obey (vi, vt)	підкоритися	[pidko'ritisʲa]
to open (vt)	відчинити	[widtʃi'niti]
to participate (vi)	брати участь	['brati 'utʃastʲ]
to pay (vi, vt)	платити	[pla'titi]
to permit (vt)	дозволяти	[dozwo'lʲati]
to play (children)	грати	['ɦrati]
to pray (vi, vt)	молитися	[mo'litisʲa]
to promise (vt)	обіцяти	[obi'tsʲati]
to propose (vt)	пропонувати	[proponu'wati]
to prove (vt)	доводити	[do'wɔditi]
to read (vi, vt)	читати	[tʃi'tati]
to receive (vt)	отримати	[ot'rimati]
to rent (sth from sb)	наймати	[naj'mati]
to repeat (say again)	повторювати	[pow'tɔrʲuwati]
to reserve, to book	резервувати	[rɛzɛrwu'wati]
to run (vi)	бігти	['biɦti]
to save (rescue)	рятувати	[rʲatu'wati]
to say (~ thank you)	сказати	[ska'zati]
to see (vt)	бачити	['batʃiti]
to sell (vt)	продавати	[proda'wati]
to send (vt)	відправляти	[widpraw'lʲati]
to shoot (vi)	стріляти	[stri'lʲati]
to shout (vi)	кричати	[kri'tʃati]
to show (vt)	показувати	[po'kazuwati]
to sign (document)	підписувати	[pid'pisuwati]
to sing (vi)	співати	[spi'wati]
to sit down (vi)	сідати	[si'dati]
to smile (vi)	посміхатися	[posmi'hatisʲa]
to speak (vi, vt)	розмовляти	[rozmow'lʲati]
to steal (money, etc.)	красти	['krasti]
to stop (please ~ calling me)	припиняти	[pripi'nʲati]
to study (vt)	вивчати	[wiw'tʃati]
to swim (vi)	плавати	['plawati]
to take (vt)	брати	['brati]
to talk to …	розмовляти з …	[rozmow'lʲati z]
to tell (story, joke)	розповідати	[rozpowi'dati]
to thank (vt)	дякувати	['dʲakuwati]
to think (vi, vt)	думати	['dumati]
to translate (vt)	перекладати	[pɛrɛkla'dati]
to trust (vt)	довіряти	[dowi'rʲati]
to try (attempt)	намагатися	[nama'hatisʲa]

| to turn (e.g., ~ left) | повертати | [powɛr'tati] |
| to turn off | вимикати | [wimi'kati] |

to turn on	вмикати	[wmi'kati]
to understand (vt)	розуміти	[rozu'miti]
to wait (vt)	чекати	[tʃɛ'kati]
to want (wish, desire)	хотіти	[ho'titi]
to work (vi)	працювати	[pratsʲu'wati]
to write (vt)	писати	[pi'sati]

Lightning Source UK Ltd.
Milton Keynes UK
UKHW020929180522
403142UK00006B/574